Embracing Crowns for Your Family

Crowned for Battle, Called to Bless:
A Kingdom Approach to Family Intercession

By

Dr. Ron M. Horner

Embracing Crowns for Your Family

Crowned for Battle, Called to Bless:
A Kingdom Approach to Family Intercession

By

Dr. Ron M. Horner

LifeSpring Publishing
PO Box 5847
Pinehurst, North Carolina 28374 USA
www.RonHorner.com

Embracing Crowns for Your Family

Crowned for Battle, Called to Bless: A Kingdom Approach to Family Intercession

Copyright © 2025 Dr. Ron M. Horner

Scripture is taken from the New King James Version®. Copyright © 1982 by Thomas Nelson. Used with permission. All rights reserved. (Unless otherwise noted.)

Scripture quotations marked (NASB) are taken from the NEW AMERICAN STANDARD BIBLE®, Copyright© 1960, 1962, 1963, 1968, 1971, 1972, 1973, 1975, 1977, 1995 by The Lockman Foundation. Used by permission.

Scripture quotations marked (NLT) are taken from the Holy Bible, New Living Translation, copyright ©1996, 2004, 2015 by Tyndale House Foundation. Used by permission of Tyndale House Publishers, Carol Stream, Illinois 60188. All rights reserved.

Scripture marked (THE MIRROR) is taken from The Mirror Study Bible by Francois du Toit. Copyright © 2021 All Rights Reserved. Used by permission of The Author.

Scripture quotations marked (TPT) is taken from The Passion Translation®. Copyright ©2017, 2018 by Passion and Fire Ministries, Inc. Used by permission. All rights reserved. The PassionTranslation.com.

All rights reserved. This book is protected by the copyright laws of the United States of America. This book may not be copied or reprinted for commercial gain or profit. The use of short quotations or occasional page copying for personal, or group study is permitted and encouraged. Permission will be granted upon request.

Trademarks are the property of their respective owners.

Requests for bulk sales discounts, editorial permissions, or other information should be addressed to:

LifeSpring Publishing
PO Box 5847
Pinehurst, NC 28374 USA

Additional copies available at: www.ronhorner.com

ISBN 13 TP: 978-1-953684-75-2
ISBN 13 eBook: 978-1-953684-76-9

Cover Design by Darian Horner Design
(www.darianhorner.com)
Image: 123rf.com #85093814

First Edition: July 2025

10 9 8 7 6 5 4 3 2 1 0

Printed in the United States of America

Table of Contents

Acknowledgments i

Characters Mentioned iii

Preface v

Chapter 1 Laying the Foundation 1

Chapter 2 Your Crown of Authority............................. 11

Chapter 3 Factors in Family Intercession................... 19

Chapter 4 Crowns for the Family Unit........................ 49

Chapter 5 Basic Categories of Wickedness 55

Chapter 6 The False Crown of Deception 59

Chapter 7 The False Crown of Loathing 85

Chapter 8 The False Crown of Fear........................... 105

Chapter 9 The False Crown of Magic 123

Chapter 10 The False Crown of Secrets 143

Chapter 11 The False Crown of Antichrist................ 163

Chapter 12 The False Crown of Devouring............... 185

Chapter 13 Gaining Freedom From False Crowns.... 205

Chapter 14 Superior Crowns 211

Chapter 15 Strategies of Hell Against Crowns........... 217

Chapter 16 Retrieving Lost Crowns 221

Chapter 17 Crown of Communion 229

Chapter 18 Helpful Assistance 235

Chapter 19 Fruit Inspectors... 241

Chapter 20 Maintaining Your Crown......................... 247

Chapter 21 Epilogue.. 255

Appendix 257

Learning to Live Spirit First 259

Resources from LifeSpring... 267

Description 273

About the Author 275

Other Books by Dr. Ron M. Horner........................... 277

Acknowledgments

Almost daily, Stephanie and I engaged Heaven concerning the crown's revelation. We knew it was vital and timely for the Body of Christ. As the sons move further into their sonship, the revelation of the crowns will be even more critical.

I wish to thank Stephanie for always being willing to engage Heaven for revelation. I honor the gift within her and bless her.

I bless my lovely wife, Adina, for her contributions and ongoing support. Thank you.

———— ∞ ————

Characters Mentioned

Adina – Dr. Ron Horner's beautiful wife, co-founder, and Chief Financial Officer of LifeSpring

John the Revelator – a man in white who wrote Revelation.

Malcolm – a man in white who tutors us in the things of Heaven.

Stephanie – serves as the Chief Operating Officer of LifeSpring International Ministries, Inc.

———— ∞ ————

Preface

The basic unit of government is the family. Heaven designed this to provide safe environments for children to be raised and learn the basics of survival and thriving in the world outside their home.

When the family government is rooted in faith in God, it has the strongest opportunity to create an environment of peace in which the family can grow. Children should be the natural outgrowth of the intimacy of a man and woman committed to one another within the bonds of the marriage covenant. In Isaiah 9:7, we read:

> *Of the **increase of His government and peace**, there will be no end, upon the throne of David and over His kingdom, to order it and establish it with judgment and justice from that time forward, even forever. The zeal of the Lord of hosts will perform this. (Emphasis mine)*

The more prominent God's government in a family unit, the more God's peace will reign in that environment. When you see a home with a lot of turmoil, it is an indication that the correct governance of the home and its atmosphere is missing.

Years ago, we had some friends whose home was always in turmoil. When you entered their home, televisions were blaring in every room, with each competing with the one in the neighboring room to be heard. Too many voices were speaking in that home. A television drama might be playing in one room, while a football game might be on in the next. With so many voices all trying to be heard, the government of that home was surrendering to the voices emanating from the electronics within the home.

A principle of government is that you will make the wrong choices if you have the wrong voices.

Wrong voices, wrong choices

Another principle of government is wrong alignments. If you have watched television or movies in the last few years, you will have noticed that they have strategically built narratives that present fathers in a family unit as just this side of useless. They are presented as dimwits, bumbling idiots, or worse. This has been strategic on the part of Satan to mock the father role and create a dishonoring of the role fathers are designed to play by Heaven. By extension, he was mocking our Heavenly Father.

In addition to the media onslaught, government policies have penalized families with a father in the home—particularly when the man and wife are married. Financial penalties were put in place to enforce this narrative.

Fathers are to be the top-tier expression of government in the home, working alongside their wives. They are responsible for demonstrating the love of the Heavenly Father to the children and to others who observe them. They are to love and cherish their wives and love and guide the children, teaching the boys to respect the females in the home and always honor them.

Mothers are to honor and respect their husbands and work as a team in raising the children. Fathers are not to lord their position over their wives or children; the wife must honor and show proper respect to the husband, modeling how we should honor and respect our Heavenly Father.

Arguments should be kept to a bare minimum, as the husband values the wife and the wife the husband. Neither parent should abuse the other or the children verbally or physically. That is not the example that our Father wants to see.

Little girls need to see their dads love them, cherish them, and always build their self-esteem so they grow up with a healthy respect and honor for men, allowing them to honor their husbands when the time comes properly. Dads should help their daughters become self-confident and capable young women, so they don't rely on boys for validation or try to get their self-worth validated by their feminine traits, nor should young men seek validation from women.

Boys need to see dads who can teach them to honor and love their moms and grow into Godly men who understand the value and worth of supporting their family through honest labor. They should always be taught to respect women and not view them as a means to self-satisfaction. Women are not objects for men's pleasure. God beautifully designs them to bring forth balance to society and the essence of love to the family.

What we have seen in society is a concerted effort to steal crowns from fathers, mothers, and children. The church bears responsibility for not enforcing Biblical mandates concerning the home and bowing to societal pressure to honor same sex marriages and transgender lifestyles as if they were the God-intended norm. They are not.

As the family unit begins to retrieve the crowns reserved for the sons, a return to Biblical government can start to occur. As dads regain their crowns, new respect and honor can come to the men. As mothers regain their authority, new honor and respect can come to them, and as children gain or regain their autonomy, new balance can come to the family unit, which will impact society. We have our work cut out for us, but when will we start if we don't start now? I suggest today.

———— ∞ ————

Chapter 1
Laying the Foundation

As designed by our Heavenly Father, a human's first point of contact is through their parents. That is why the enemy has roared like a lion. We must destroy what he has been doing and be empowered to re-establish this in people's lives.

Proverbs 1:8-9:

> *8 Hear my son, your father's instruction and do not forsake your mother's teaching.... 9 Indeed, they are a graceful wreath to your head, **a crown** and ornaments about your neck. A mantle. (NASB) (Emphasis mine)*

Dealing with Deficiencies

We must address any deficiencies regarding our ability to give and receive love from parents to make the progress Heaven has in mind throughout the rest of our lives. Remember that parents cannot give you what they don't possess themselves. That has been the situation for many people.

When we engaged Heaven and were taught about mantles, which are a part of every crown, Malcolm, our tutor, spoke of having a chip on our shoulders due to disappointments and disillusionment that we have experienced throughout our lives, particularly concerning parents and caregivers. For some, we need to let our parents or caregivers off the hook. Children have this instruction concerning their parents found in Ephesians 6:1-4:

> *[1] Children, obey your parents in the Lord, for this is right. [2] 'Honor your father and mother,' which is the first commandment with promise: [3] 'That it may be well with you and you may live long on the earth.' [4] And you, fathers, do not provoke your children to wrath, but bring them up in the training and admonition of the Lord.*

Another arena we must deal with is the possible chip on our shoulder. That chip could be offense or dishonor, among many other things. A definition of this idiom is found in the Merriam-Webster Dictionary:

: to have an angry or unpleasant attitude or way of behaving caused by a belief that one has been treated unfairly in the past[1]

Example: He has had a chip on his shoulder ever since he didn't get the Xbox he was expecting.

Mantles cannot land when we have a chip on our shoulder. We must remove the chips so the mantle can land. Some of that is as simple as forgiving, blessing, and releasing the offender.

There are mantles to be picked up like crowns. Often, an offense will present itself when a mantle is about to fall upon us. We must deal with the chip first.

*The enemy is afraid of crowns,
but he's more fearful of the mantles.*

*Remember, with crowns,
you walk in your authority,
with the mantles,
you assert your authority.*

---

[1] Merriam-Webster, "Have a chip on one's shoulder," Accessed February 25, 2025.

The Mantle of Receiving Love from Your Parents

The children can receive a mantle of Receiving Love from Your Parents. Many children had this one knocked off their shoulders, or it couldn't land early in their lives. This is a special mantle for children to carry. The love that is supposed to be given by the parents is in this mantle. With this mantle, you can walk in the surety, and the receiving of the love of a father and of a mother that is healthy and pure. It's a mantle of comfort. Many don't have this mantle, but the Lord can restore all.

Stephanie prayed:

Father, I thank You for this mantle and ask to step back in time to when I was to receive this mantle from You. I know it was given to me at birth, too, and I had that mantle. I see that it was on me as a baby, but here it's as if this mantle had outgrown the other one, and the new one was to be established, and I missed it, or it came off my shoulders because of a chip.

[You may need to pause and pray a similar prayer.]

Think about this. This mantle is being hindered from landing because of a chip on your shoulder. Maintaining a mantle of a parent's love and comfort would be difficult if you no longer trust it. You must let it be reestablished in you. With it will come the comfort and the love—a reestablishment of that parental love. The children whose parents gave them away are missing this mantle.

This mantle is essential because receiving love from anyone is very difficult without it. Many hold others at arm's length. Many have difficulty being parents and refuse the Father's love. So have it reestablished.

With a crown comes a mantle. When you receive a crown, you are also receiving its mantle.

Stephanie prayed:

I ask to step into the Court of Crowns to receive my Crown of Parental Love and Comfort, my mantle, and the authority that comes with it.

I ask that it be reestablished in my life.

How does this work for those who were adopted or whose parents may have let them live with them, but they abused them? It is the same. This is for their healing. This is for their reestablishment and to feel like a human, to experience love.

We cannot do this without forgiving all who have deeply wounded us. That is why we cannot have a chip on our shoulders.

Stephanie again prayed:

Father, I pray that many will be reestablished into wholeness from this mantle being placed back on the shoulders and this Crown of Nurture and Being Nurtured.

This is so valuable, especially for so many who lost a parent in childbirth, whose parents gave them away, or who lived in abusive, horrific situations where this was supposed to be their **first understanding of love through a parent**. It is a wrap-around love.

Psalms 32:10:

*But when you trust in the Lord for forgiveness, **his wrap-around love will surround you.** (TPT) (Emphasis mine)*

Psalms 61:3:

*Lord, You are a paradise of protection to me. You lift me high above the fray. None of my foes can touch me when **I'm held firmly in your wrap-around presence!** (TPT) (Emphasis mine)*

Some say, "I know the Father loves me, but I can't experience it." That is a mantle that has been lost. The crown is gone because parents are supposed to give A picture of the Father's love in an unconditional, loving manner towards a newborn and children.

Parents are to provide
an environment of unconditional
love for their children.

Pray this:

I request access to the Court of Crowns.

Thank You, Father, for this Crown of Nurture and Being Nurtured, and for this mantle.

I ask for an establishment of all mantles for the crowns I have received to date to be placed upon my shoulder in this wrap-around love that I feel here in this court—the authority that it gives us and the reestablishment.

I forgive those in my life who failed to provide me with nurture and care. I bless them and release them now, in Jesus' name.

Thank You, Your Honor.

You may need to prophetically place a mantle like this upon your parents' shoulders. Because you have received it, you can give it like Peter and John in the Book of Acts, when they said, 'Silver and gold, I don't have, but what I do have, I give to you.'[2]

To the parents who did not have this, say to them:

I give you this because I know you missed out on this, too.

---

[2] Acts 3:6

I ask for him/her to have a Crown of Nurture put back on his/her head.

[You may want to pray a similar prayer for your parents or caregivers.]

Colossians 3:21 says,

> *Fathers do not provoke your children less they become discouraged.*

Or, as one translation says:

> *And fathers, don't have unrealistic expectations for your children or else they may become discouraged. (TPT)*

2 Timothy 1:5:

> *For I am mindful of the sincere faith within you, which first dwelt in your grandmother Lois and your mother Eunice, and I'm sure that is in you as well.*

Proverbs 1:8-9:

> *⁸ Hear my son, your father's instruction and do not forsake your mother's teaching.... ⁹ Indeed, they are a graceful wreath to your head, **a crown** and ornaments about your neck. A mantle. (NASB) (Emphasis mine)*

1 Thessalonians 2:7-8:

> *⁷ But we proved to be gentle among you **as a nursing mother, tenderly caring for her own children.** ⁸ Having so fond an affection for you, we were well pleased to impart to you not only the gospel of God, but also our own lives. (Emphasis mine)*

Stephanie prayed:

Thank You, Lord, for this crown and this mantle. You are helping me reestablish how to receive love from You and be healed from childhood wounds and the chips on my shoulders, so that the mantles can fall upon me properly.

Help me better understand the mantles that come with crowns and the ones on the ground that I need to retrieve. Give us insight; give us instruction. Open the eyes of my understanding.

As mentioned earlier, receiving these crowns is essential to giving and receiving love adequately. They help provide us with a foundation for later in life. Where we missed this, where these crowns might have been lost or stolen, step back into the Court of Crowns and request their restoration in your life.

Ask for the amendment of "As if it Never Were" and step into the newness of your life, having been loved and now being able to receive and give love.

False Mantles

Many don't recognize that just as you can receive Godly mantles into your life, false crowns will manifest false mantles, causing you to exhibit the wrong things. Some parents may have received a false mantle of a perverted expectation of their children where the children are trophies, or glorified slaves to the parents, and they are not loved and nurtured as was the Father's plan.

Just as Godly crowns have mantles, so do false crowns and ungodly crowns.

We want their removal. When you recognize you have received a false crown, repent and request the removal of the false crown and any false mantle you may have received. Don't live under the expression of ANY false crown. It's time to step into who you truly are, not a counterfeit version your enemy has sought to impose on your life. You have a place of rest from which to begin to operate. It's time to take a seat.

———— ∞ ————

Chapter 2
Your Crown of Authority

In this engagement, the scene was a cosmic one.[3] They showed her the background. She could see different cosmic dimensions, and Ezekiel stood in front of what we would view as a star, a brightly lit star. He took his sword and pierced it. It was the Bright and Morning Star. As he did so, a liquid poured forth that appeared pure in its form, with gold and white elements flowing out. As it poured out, the star seemed to collapse.

Ezekiel moved up to a host of other angels that Stephanie began to see. There were millions and millions of angels. She realized that the liquid pouring from the star was falling onto the earth and into the crowns on their heads. As the last drops of liquid from

---

[3] This chapter taken from *Embracing Your Crown of Authority* by Dr. Ron M. Horner, LifeSpring Publishing (2025)

the star fell onto the Earth, they covered the entire planet. She could hear a shout that the angels had shouted as they came full force towards the earth. She could see them piercing the atmosphere as they fought in the heavens. She could see from the perspective on earth that we, the sons, with these crowns filled with oil—this light and gold—had our hands outstretched, and we were praying and speaking to the atmosphere with authority, as if the words we spoke empowered the angels.

We had just seen an illustration of how these crowns are vessels upon our heads. Supernatural outpourings go into these crowns, each unique to the individual.

Although we may have crowns with the same name, what is poured out to the individual and upon their head, filling the crown, is unique to that individual. This is a picture of the uniqueness of each crown: the outpouring and the infilling of Jesus into the crown. Just as unique as each person's relationship with the Trinity, so is the uniqueness of what is poured out to the individual.

A diversity among the crowns exists as well as a diversity of the outpouring.

If each of you carried the same anointing, there would be no use for the body. Discover what has been poured out. The discovery is in the unique intimacy with the Trinity. Jesus, who has poured himself out, is one piece of this.

What do you carry?

View this in the aspect of the crown on your head, for we know it is not in and of yourselves, but what He has given. See the perspective from the crown. These are the mysteries that are being unfolded to the sons.

Ask what the uniqueness is that you carry in your crown? Ask the Trinity—the Father, Son, and Holy Spirit, "What is the unique pouring out you have put in my crown?"

The Holy Spirit will give you a unique personalization, the Father will give you specific authorization, and Jesus will provide you with a specific organization (on how to manifest it on earth).

Ask, "How is it unique for the Kingdom?"

- Pause and ask the Trinity: "What is your unique outpouring for my crown?"
- Pause and ask the Father: "What is the unique authorization of my Crown of Authority?"
- Ask Jesus: "What is the specific organization of my Crown of Authority?"
- And ask Holy Spirit: "What is the unique personalization of my Crown of Authority?"

[If necessary, pause and pray in the spirit before and after each question. These are some of the mysteries Heaven is revealing currently.]

The crown on top of your head is filled with liquid that contains the components necessary for authorization, personalization, and organization of that crown. As you live, move, and have your being in Jesus, you walk in this authorization, organization, and unique personalization. It spills out of this crown. Do you know how, when you walk with a cup of coffee, it's too full and spills over? It looks like that. This is *your* Crown of Authority.

It is because it's not our authority.
This is a picture OF authority.

The authority in *and from* this crown is *unique to each person.*

Every person walks in
a specific authority that is different
and unique from others.

Everyone has a Crown of Authority.

It is what is being poured into that crown, be it from hell or Heaven, that is unique to the individual, also.

What are you making your source to draw from?

Princes and the powers of this earth pour out a vile liquid into the Crowns of Authority of those who walk in darkness.

The reason you have a Crown of Authority from the moment of your birth is *because you are <u>from</u> and <u>out of</u> the Father*.

---
*You are from and out of
His original creation,
uniqueness, and design.*

See yourself as a baby with this little crown on your head. That's what the enemy seeks to defile—this specific Crown of Authority with Christ is placed on us at birth. We rule and reign.

---
*The enemy seeks to defile
this specific Crown of Authority.*

---
*If the crown can be defiled,
it removes the authority of the sons.*

> *Satan fears when we walk
> with the heavenly anointing
> poured into the crown's authority.*

We are part of changing the Earth, part of assisting angels, part of it all. We are kings and priests.

We can be kings and priests for the Kingdom of Heaven or the kingdom of darkness. Satan fell because he saw us in the future and was extremely upset about it. He was upset about our authority, which is more than he has.

> *We have more authority than Satan.*

Hebrews 1:5-6:

> [5] *For to which of the angels did He ever say: 'You are my son, today I have begotten you?' And again: 'I will be to him a Father, and he shall be to me a son?'*
>
> [6] *But when He again brings the firstborn into the world, He says: 'Let all the angels of God worship Him.'*

> *God never gave authority to angels,
> like he has given to His sons.*

Satan did not like his job placement as the lead worshipper in Heaven. He wanted the authority the sons had. That dissatisfaction resulted in the rebellion, during which one-third of the angels fell.

What we say in the spiritual realm truly does matter, and it assists the angels in many ways. They have great strength, and they do things, but *we* carry the authority.

Revelation 3:11:

> **Remember that you call the shots, you wear the crown. My crown endorses your crown. Let nothing take your crown.** *(MIRROR) (Emphasis mine)*

For anyone who believes they are too small or have done too much wrong, *the crown came from the Father when He created us* and when we choose to be filled with the goodness of the Bright and Morning Star. The authority that He has given us, we don't ever have to worry about that again. Let's pray:

I request access to the Court of Crowns.

I request that my Crown of Authority be filled with the goodness of the Bright and Morning Star.

Isaiah 53:5:

> But he was **pierced for our rebellion (transgression)**, crushed for our sins. He was

beaten so we could be whole. He was whipped so we could be healed.. (Emphasis mine)

He was pierced. What he did created this anointing for all of the sons.

This is your original design.

The pouring out is celestial, supernatural, and dimensional, and it's a picture of the unique authorization and filling of our crowns to walk in the authority, boldness, and execution of our sonship on this earth.

Thank You, Heaven. Thank You, Father, and thank You, Jesus. I ask that for every person that hears this message and they ask for the mystery for themselves, the uniqueness of what you have poured into their Crown of Authority, that they are empowered in their heart and their mind realizing that this lie that we've all believed that we have no authority is dismantled forever.

Thank You, Jesus, that you were poured out and overcame our transgressions so we might walk in authority as sons. Thank you..

——— ∞ ———

Chapter 3
Factors in Family Intercession

Recognizing the common enemies every part of a family faces is essential to overcoming the onslaughts that come into our lives. Here is a short list of items to deal with in the Courts of Heaven on behalf of the husbands, wives, and children for whom we should pray regularly:

- Accusations
- False Verdicts
- Ungodly Bonds
- Covenants
- Corruption
- Corrupted Crowns
- LHS involvement
- Ungodly Trades
- Evil altars
- Freemasonry

Parents should look for clues from their children concerning the accusations they face. Imagine how many accusations they face daily from school situations, friends, and family members. Many of these accusations can be unveiled in conversations with your children. In other cases, step into the Court of Records and ask what accusations you need to get mantled in the Courts of Heaven.

For false verdicts, think of how many false verdicts they have to contend with. Again, the Court of Records has the information on what false verdicts are on the docket against your family. Living under false verdicts creates immense pressure on one's psyche. Do similarly for your spouse.

What about ungodly bonds? We must also address those who impact our spouse and children. Placing Godly bonds of wisdom, fortitude, courage, hope, unity, peace, wholeness, and more would benefit those in your family.

We have discussed the corruption of the office and the seat of power that must be repented for on behalf of the current occupants.

We must also consider the corruption of the crowns of those in the family. Whether the crowns have been stolen, lost, forfeited, or corrupted in some manner, our families need them restored so they can enjoy the full benefits of those crowns.

Then, how many ungodly covenants are in play that are working against your family? These could be generational covenants, covenants related to your family directly, or those against your neighborhood, and so on.

You also have to consider the corruption of the roles of the father, mother, or children. Just as you can have corruption in a political office and in the seat of that office, you can also have corruption in each seat in a family unit.

A further dynamic to consider is the involvement of lingering human spirits in the lives of the individuals and their realms. What if LHSs were involved in causing the turmoil in your home this morning? Could LHSs have been on assignment to cause such a thing to occur? Or do you have LHSs who simply want to go home and are trying to get your attention?

What if you had the spirit of a deceased grandparent, aunt, or uncle who missed the position he or she once had? Would they be willing to give up that position and transition into Heaven?

What if someone in their former position was hosting them and was a dominant influence in their life? These LHSs need to be removed so that each part of the family can fulfill their roles without such influence.

It would not be surprising to find LHSs involved in many activities against families—yours included. We commonly find that grandma is still hanging out with one of the kids or grandkids, long after her passing. The influence of these lingering human spirits cannot be ignored. Not every ministry understands this concept, but those who have followed LifeSpring are aware that we fully embrace it and regularly teach about it.

The last item on my list to consider (but not the last possible option) is the regular, ungodly trades within families. With children, electronics, online games, and the like seem to be unhealthy trades that hinder and affect families. They need to be canceled and their effects neutralized.

In the following few pages, we will provide some patterns for dealing with each of these items I have listed and cover these areas more thoroughly.

As sons, Heaven is teaching us how to use our authority more effectively to accomplish things for the Kingdom of Heaven. When accomplishing family intercession and before dealing with any of the factors, follow these steps:

1. Firmly place the Crown of Family on your head.
2. Take your seat on the throne of Family Intercession.
3. Pause
4. Pray in the spirit.
5. Call your angels near.
6. Commission them to co-labor with the governmental angels of your family.

7. Ask for the strategies of Heaven to be unveiled to you today.
8. Begin the work.

Accusations

Since the first family existed, the family unit has been subject to an onslaught of accusations. Some of the accusations may contain some truth, but many do not. The same thing happens to us. We experience accusations daily. The volume of accusations the family unit faces is hard to fathom. The following passage says it well.

2 Corinthians 2:11:

> *The agenda of **any accusation** is to **divide** and **dominate**. (MIRROR) (Emphasis mine)*

If I can get you to embrace an accusation (particularly a false one), I can begin to divide you from the truth about the situation. Once I have divided you from the truth about a matter, I have then redefined how you view that person and will begin to dominate that relationship. If you believe every accusation against your spouse and do not seek out the truth about an issue, that accusation will eventually dominate your thinking about your spouse.

We don't have to always agree with our spouse or children, but we need to deal with accusations on their behalf so that they can function on a more level playing field. We follow the same pattern when dealing with accusations against him as when dealing with accusations against ourselves, our spouse, our children, or anyone else.

The steps are:

1. Agree with the adversary quickly.
2. Confess it as a sin.
3. Repent.
4. Ask the blood of Jesus to be applied to that accusation and all the ramifications of it.

In just a few moments, you will have dismantled that accusation from having power over the other person's life. You will have done them a tremendous favor.

Court Scenario

Concerning Accusations Against a Spouse

I request access to the realms of Heaven and the Court of Mercy on behalf of my spouse.

Your Honor, I present the application, which states that my spouse is accused of __(list the accusation here)__.

On their behalf, I agree with the adversary, I confess it as sin, I repent on their behalf, and ask that the blood of

Jesus be applied to this accusation and all the ramifications of it.

Your Honor, I await your righteous verdict or further counsel.

[Await the verdict or further counsel.]

[If further counsel is warranted, follow the leading of Holy Spirit and the court until you receive a righteous verdict. Further repentance may be required. Once the verdict is granted, thank the court and exit.]

Concerning Accusations Against Your Child

I request access to the realms of Heaven and the Court of Mercy on behalf of my child(ren).

Your Honor, I present the accusation that my child is a __(list the accusation here)__ .

On their behalf, I agree with the adversary; I confess it as sin, I repent on their behalf, and ask that the blood of Jesus be applied to this accusation and all its ramifications.

Your Honor, I await your righteous verdict or further counsel.

[Await the verdict or further counsel.]

[If further counsel is warranted, follow the leading of Holy Spirit and the court until you receive a righteous verdict. Further repentance may be required. Once the verdict is granted, thank the court and exit.]

Dealing with these accusations regularly would be helpful to your spouse and children. Without the accusations hanging over one's head, they will be much more able to hear the Lord's voice and act righteously.

False Verdicts

Accusations *affect* behavior; false verdicts can *dictate* behavior. For example, a false verdict of "he can never do anything right" will create the behavior the false verdict espouses. Anyone can have an encounter with Heaven and experience change. It need not be a presupposed belief that if you are the husband or wife, you must do wicked deeds or put wicked rules in place. You want false verdicts replaced with righteous verdicts on behalf of the person the false verdict is about, because how that person behaves affects us all.

Court Scenario

I request access to the Court of Appeals in Heaven on behalf of my spouse/my son/daughter. I present the false verdict of _____.

Your Honor, I repent for the sins of my spouse/my son/daughter. I forgive, bless, and release them, as instructed in John 20:23.

I ask that this false verdict be overturned and replaced with a righteous verdict.

I ask for Your verdict or further counsel.

[Await the verdict or further counsel.]

[If further counsel is warranted, follow the leading of Holy Spirit and the court until you receive a righteous verdict. Again, more repentance may be required. Once the verdict is granted, thank the court and exit.]

Ungodly Bonds

Your family is undoubtedly affected by ungodly bonds, some of which arise from people's words, the counsels of hell, or the activities of lingering spirits on assignment against your family. As sons, we need to break these ungodly bonds and replace them with godly ones, so that your family can function more freely and righteously.

Not everyone in your family may currently have a heart for God or the things of God, but they can be a person God is using at this hour, and they can hear from Him. They will hear a lot better if the saints in the family pray more effectively for him/her rather than complain about them.

Every complaint is worship to the adversary. We don't want to empower the adversary by our complaints. Instead of complaints coming from the mouth of the sons, instead we need to be releasing righteous declarations that everyone in your family has a heart that is tender toward the Lord and sees the hand of God protecting them physically, emotionally, and spiritually and that God is granting them wisdom to position your family for great blessing. That should be our declaration over our family members and similar declarations. The sons can do better than they have in times past.

In our court work regarding family intercession, we will use a recently released authority and revelation called the Strike Force Method. Once an ungodly bond is recognized (or a series of them), stand in your positional place as a son, take the quill of the Lord in your hand, and strike through every ungodly bond. You can strike through these bonds, eliminating them quickly. An example of a ~~strikethrough is this~~. Then, request that Heaven be invoked for the Godly bonds to be placed upon their bond registry.

Court Scenario

I request access to the Court of Records on behalf of my spouse/my children.

I request a listing of the ungodly bonds on every page of their Bond Registry.

As a son, in agreement with Heaven, I take the quill of the Lord and strike through every ungodly bond placed upon their life.

I request the placement of Godly bonds upon his registry on every page.

Thank you, Your Honor.

Covenants

Many times, when dealing with situations in people's lives, there seems to be little breakthrough. I have found that an ungodly covenant is often involved, usually from the person's ancestors. Someone hundreds of years ago may have come into a covenant of death of some flavor that has impacted that generation and every generation since. Repentance for the implementation of that covenant must be done so that the person can be free to function and live under the blessing of a covenant of life.

Court Scenario

I request access to the Court of Cancellations on behalf of my spouse/son/daughter. I ask that every covenant made throughout their generations, whether on the paternal side or the maternal side, be brought forth.

Your Honor, I repent on behalf of my spouse/son/daughter and on behalf of their generations for making covenants that were out of keeping with Your will for their life and that of their family. I forgive, bless, and release all who did these things. They probably did not know what they were doing.

I ask that these covenants be voided and destroyed this day. I ask that they be burned with the fire of the Lord. I ask that every taxation resulting from these covenants be lifted from their lives, the lives of their families, and their generations.

I ask that you implement a covenant of life in their life and on behalf of them and those related to them by blood, marriage, adoption, civil, or religious covenant.

I await your verdict of further counsel, Your Honor.

[Await the verdict or further counsel.]

[If further counsel is warranted, follow the leading of Holy Spirit and the court until you receive a righteous verdict. Once the verdict is granted, thank the court and exit.]

Corruption

Throughout history, the family unit has been plagued by corruption. This could take the form of a wandering eye of a marriage partner or the wrong relationships, which can be on the parental or children's side. It has affected the family and all those who are part of it.

We need to repent for the corruption within the family and in each family member's seat, so that the corruption does not pass to the children. Corruption, to some degree, has tried to rear its ugly head in many places, but that is not a reason to excuse it. As sons, our responsibility is to repent of it and allow the cleansing power of the Kingdom of Heaven to work in that situation.

Have the angelic cleaning crews clean up the spiritual debris left by corruption and root out all corruption on every level, in every position, and wherever it is found, uprooting, burning out, and destroying it. We want to leave future generations in much better shape than we are currently in.

Court Scenario

I request access to the Court of the Family.

Your Honor, I stand here as a father/mother/son/daughter(adjust as needed) in repentance for every level of corruption within our family and generations.

I repent for my sins, the sins of my father, mother, brothers, and sisters, and every wicked deed performed by the men and women in our family throughout the generations.

I repent for every sin they have committed. According to John 20:23, as a son, I forgive their sins, bless them, and release them.

I ask that angels be dispatched to uncover every bit of corruption in our family line and to eradicate it. I ask that justice be done according to Your laws.

I ask for a cleansing of our family and our family name from every vestige of corruption.

I request that angels be assigned to police this office and keep out those who would bring corruption to our family.

I ask that you empower Mom, Dad, and our children to resist and hate every form of corruption so that it may be rooted out, and this family can be righteous according to Your design, Your Honor.

I await your verdict of further counsel, Your Honor.

[Await the verdict or further counsel.]

[If further counsel is warranted, follow the leading of Holy Spirit and the court until you receive a righteous verdict. Once the verdict is granted, thank the court and exit.]

Corrupted Crowns

We also know that crowns can be corrupted, so the Crown of Parental Leadership upon the mother and father must also be cleansed. The same cleansing must be done for every crown among each family member.

---

*If the crown can be defiled,
it removes the authority of the sons.*

---

*Satan fears when we walk
with the heavenly anointing
poured into the crown's authority.*

Court Scenario

I request access to the Court of Crowns.

Your Honor, I stand here as a citizen of the United States (adjust as needed) in repentance for every crown that has been corrupted within our family.

I repent for our sins and those before us. I repent for every wicked deed performed by the fathers and mothers in our generations.

I repent for those seeking to steal, destroy, or corrupt the crowns granted to us by Heaven.

I repent for their greed, for their lust for power, for their adulterous behavior, for their graft, for every sin they have committed. As a son, according to John 20:23, I forgive their sins, bless them, and release them.

I ask that angels be dispatched to recover every lost, stolen, or forfeited crown and uncover every corruption of the crowns in these offices within the family unit. I ask that they destroy every bit of corruption. I ask that justice be done according to Your laws.

I ask for cleansing the Crown of Parental Leadership from every vestige of corruption.

I request the cleansing of every crown corrupted among our children.

I ask for the restoration of every lost crown and its components in our family.

I request that angels be assigned to police these offices and keep out those who would bring corruption in their crowns.

I ask that you empower each family member to resist and reject every form of corruption so that it may be rooted out, and our family can be righteous according to Your design, Your Honor. Empower us to guard the crowns that we wear.

I await your verdict or further counsel, Your Honor.

[Await the verdict or further counsel.]

[If further counsel is warranted, follow the leading of Holy Spirit and the court until you receive a righteous verdict. Once the verdict is granted, thank the court and exit.]

Lingering Human Spirit Involvement

It has been our experience that lingering human spirits (the spirits of those who have died but have not yet transitioned to Heaven or hell) wander the dry places. Sometimes, they find their abode with someone living. They typically prefer the family unit they came from. At times, these lingering spirits are compelled by dark forces to commit heinous acts against others. They can affect people, offices, atmospheres, and even nations. Remember the woman in the Bible with the "spirit" of infirmity. That was not a demon, but it was a lingering human spirit forced to introduce infirmity into the woman's body so that she was constantly suffering and never able to get well.

For example, we dealt with the LHS in a young man who worked as a handyman. His father had been in the construction industry. He requested that we check his realms for any lingering human spirit and detected his father, who had died a few years prior, was present.

We helped his father transition to Heaven, and the young man sensed release. However, a few days later, he noticed he no longer had the expertise to fix things like he once did. His wife told us he no longer knew how to change a doorknob. His expertise was from his father's knowledge base, not his own.

Thankfully, he was a licensed electrical contractor, so he returned to that line of work as being a handyman was no longer an option.

When an LHS is removed from someone's realms, that person can begin to think more clearly and, in some cases, discover who they are without the interference that an LHS can bring. That is why we want the thought processes to clear up and come into proper balance.

Many times, we have dealt with instances where grandma was being hosted unknowingly by a daughter or granddaughter. The granddaughter would find herself shopping for clothes more appropriate for an older person than a twenty-year-old. When grandma was able to transition to Heaven, the daughter was under no compulsion to shop for older-style clothes. She could be who she was—herself.

Registry Interference by LHSs

Sometimes, LHSs can be forced to file ungodly bonds on someone's registry. These can often be detected by their sheer vileness. Frequently, a lot of four-letter words will appear on a bond registry. That can be somewhat shocking when it's not how you usually speak.

To remove these ungodly bonds and the responsible LHSs, we will again use the Strike Force Method. First, we will use the procedure mentioned earlier to break the ungodly bonds, and then we will address the LHS that has been under assignment.

I am convinced that most LHSs under assignment from a demonic guard who is under assignment from a higher-level entity probably did not want to be coerced to do what they were doing. It is possible that some were quite willing to commit these deeds and may not have been the nicest of people when they were alive on earth in a physical body. We will address them in two ways.

For Those LHSs Forced to Participate

Court Scenario

As a son, I request access to the Court of Records.

I request that the Guest Registry be opened for _____ (name the person).

I wish to see the list of human spirits who have been forced into servitude against them.

I ask angels to gather all those human spirits and bring them here now.

Your Honor, in agreement with John 20:23, which states, 'whoever sins I remit, they are remitted to them.' I remit their sins now. I forgive, bless, and release them.

As a son, I strike their assignment and the assignment of the demonic guards and their princes. I strike every ungodly bond that has been placed against them. I commission angels to deal with the demonic guards and their bosses according to the will of Heaven.

I request that the silver channel be opened and angels usher these human spirits into the realms of Heaven. I recommend that they call on the mercy of the Lord when they stand before him.

I request that angels be assigned to clean up all spiritual debris.

I request that the silver channel be closed now.

I request angels to place Godly bonds upon their registry according to their scroll and the will of the Father.

Thank you for your assistance and for bringing clarity to their mind.

For Those LHSs Who Participated Willingly

Court Scenario

As a son, I request access to the Court of Records.

I request that the Guest Registry be opened for _____ (name the person).

I wish to see the list of human spirits who have been in servitude against them by an act of their will.

I ask angels to gather all those human spirits and bring them here now.

Your Honor, in agreement with John 20:23, which states, "whoever sins I remit, they are remitted to them." I remit their sins now. I forgive, bless, and release them.

As a son, I strike their assignment and the assignment of the demonic guards and their princes. I strike every ungodly bond that has been placed against them.

I request that the silver channel be opened and angels usher these human spirits into the realms of Heaven. I recommend that they call on the mercy of the Lord when they stand before him.

I request that angels be assigned to clean up all spiritual debris.

I request that the silver channel be closed now.

I request that Godly bonds be placed upon their Bond Registry according to their scroll and the will of the Father.

Thank you for your assistance and for bringing clarity to their mind.

For Those LHSs Being Hosted

Not all LHSs are under assignment, and they have found a comfortable abode with someone, so that we will deal with them slightly differently.

Court Scenario

As a son, I request access to the Court of Records.

I request that the Guest Registry be opened for _____ (name the person).

I wish to see the list of human spirits currently being hosted by _____, including those hiding between realms.

I ask angels to gather all those human spirits and bring them here now.

Your Honor, in agreement with John 20:23, which states, 'whoever sins I remit, they are remitted to them.' I remit their sins now. I forgive, bless, and release them.

I request that angels be assigned to clean up all spiritual debris.

I request that the silver channel be closed now.

I request angels to place Godly bonds upon _____'s Bond Registry according to his scroll and the will of the Father.

Thank you for your assistance and for bringing clarity to _____'s mind.

Ungodly Trades

Throughout the generations, many husbands have cheated on their wives, and wives have cheated on their husbands. Children have rebelled, fought, run away, gotten pregnant, and have engaged in ungodly trades to gain positions, power, prestige, riches, companionship, drugs, and more. Some even to the point of sex trafficking. The more precious the victim to the perpetrator, the more valuable the trade. Usually, blood is the currency used in making these trades, especially innocent bloodshed.

For example, someone might want more riches. They may be required to sacrifice a cat, dog, or chicken. They make the trade by killing the animal and begin to receive more money.

Of course, they are not satisfied with a bit of money. They want more, a lot more. They go to whoever was guiding them in the process, like a witch, warlock, or satanic priest, and they advise them that the next sacrifice must be larger and more significant. They decide to kill a large dog as part of their trade. They do the deed and begin accumulating more riches, but again, they are unsatisfied and want more.

Again, they are advised that more bloodshed is needed, but this time, the victim must be human—an infant or a small child, perhaps. Again, they do the deed and have the promised riches, but they are unsatisfied with what they have now. They return to their advisor, who notifies them that this sacrifice must be more precious than any others. It must be their spouse or their mother.

They may wrestle with this for a while but eventually agree to the terms of the trade and make the sacrifice. Their deeds possibly haunt them, but they are beginning to realize that enough is never enough. They are enslaved to this trading floor and the need for innocent bloodshed.

Sometimes, the innocent bloodshed can be satisfied by sex with a virgin female. Other times, it is much more violent. Sex trafficking has entrapped multiplied thousands of boys and girls of all ages, and sadly, some of our politicians are contributing to the problem. The influence the sex trafficking peddlers have on many politicians needs to be repented of, and the strategies of Heaven be invoked to see change come.

Too many scenarios exist to develop a simple Court Scenario, but I will present a reasonably generic one from which you can build.

Court Scenario

Concerning Victims

As a son, I request access to the Court of Trades. I request the spirit(s) of _____ be brought into this court.

I also request that the relevant cloud of witnesses be present, as well as the spirits of those evil advisors.

I also request the spirits of every victim to be brought into this court as well and be placed in a safe zone for these proceedings.

Your Honor, we present _____ to you as he is alleged to have sacrificed innocent bloodshed in making ungodly trades. I recognize this wickedness and repent of it on their behalf.

I repent for the innocent bloodshed.

I repent for the loss of wages.

I repent for the loss of properties and lands in making these ungodly trades.

I request that the evil entities that invoked these wicked trades be judged in this court today.

Those used, like the plaintiff here today, were deceived. We forgive them of every sin. We forgive, bless, and release them.

We ask that their corrupted Crown of Authority be cleansed, emptied of every vile thing, and made pure by Your hand.

On behalf of the victims, I request the restoration to the lives and bloodlines of the victims of these atrocious acts.

I ask angels to gather and bring those whose spirits have yet to transition to Heaven into this court.

We forgive you of every sin. I ask angels to open the silver channel and usher you to the presence of Jesus. I recommend you call upon His mercy when you stand before Him. Begin your destiny in Heaven.

We ask angels to cleanse the realms of these present from all wickedness.

We now close the silver channel.

Evil Altars

The erection of evil altars often occurs to create a platform for ungodly sacrifices and covenants to be settled. At these altars, people would worship the deity to which it was dedicated and make offerings to appease the god. This occurred many times in the Old Testament; the instruction to dismantle them was to destroy them. The prophets would sometimes tear them down piece by piece. Often, these are now spiritual places that have been erected, rather than actual physical altars. For their removal, repentance is required.

In the past, child sacrifice has been used to further the agendas of various political or business leaders. Bloodshed is a currency of hell that Satan convinces ungodly, misguided people to utilize to accomplish wicked things.

Court Scenario

I request access to the Court of Cancellations on behalf of (my spouse/my children).

I request that every evil altar be brought forward into this court along with the altar attendant(s).

Your Honor, I repent on behalf of (my spouse/my children) and behalf of our generations for erecting altars that were out of keeping with Your will for their life and that of our family. I forgive, bless, and release all who did these things. They may not have known what they were doing.

I request that these altars be dismantled and destroyed today. I ask that they be burned with the fire of the Lord. I ask that every taxation resulting from these evil altars be lifted from their life and the lives of our family and our generations.

I ask that you implement a covenant of life in their life and on behalf of those related to them by blood, marriage, adoption, civil, or religious covenant.

I await your verdict of further counsel, Your Honor.

[Await the verdict or further counsel.]

[If further counsel is warranted, follow the leading of Holy Spirit and the court until you receive a righteous verdict. Once the verdict is granted, thank the court and exit.]

Freemasonry

Embedded in the founding of many nations is the false religion of Freemasonry. Although Freemasons deny being a religion or a secret society, they are both. They have creeds, initiation rites, and their Bible. They observe a ritual of communion. They have members and seek to indoctrinate them into their religion. They even have evangelists whose job is to spread the news of Freemasonry.

Freemasonry is a pagan religion whose endgame is the worship of Lucifer. Although that, too, is denied (at least until the upper levels of Freemasonry), their constitution and creeds outline these facts. Their gospel is a message of good works on the surface. Oaths bind them to one another and the furtherance of their message and methodology. They believe their law to be superior to any other law, even the laws of the nation, and more tragically, the laws of God.

Repentance must be done for those who have engaged in this form of pagan worship. I refer to it as pagan worship with a suit. If you or anyone in your lineage has been involved in Freemasonry in any way, I have two recommendations for you to undertake immediately:

1. Read through my book *Overcoming the False Verdicts of Freemasonry: Fourth Edition*[4] and go through each court scenario,
2. Read my book and work your way through the court scenarios of *Freedom from Mithraism: Second Edition*.[5]

Everyone is impacted by Freemasonry and Mithraism (an ancient pagan religion) that has infected the church through the acts of Constantine, the former emperor.

---

[4] Available from ronhorner.com. LifeSpring Publishing (2025).

[5] LifeSpring Publishing (2021).

You cannot cast out what you have in common. Deal with it in your lineage or avoid doing court work until you have dealt with it in your life and in your generations.

To provide a court scenario for Freemasonry could take up the entire volume of this book. Utilize the principles and court scenarios of my book *Overcoming the False Verdicts of Freemasonry*.

Finally

To deal with these different factors in praying for our families honors the Father and helps bring the will of God to pass. Using these Court Scenarios will help in the process of focused intercession, which we can achieve through the paradigm of the Courts of Heaven. I have been writing on the Courts of Heaven for over nine years. As sons, we have a greater responsibility and know-how than many others. It is time we put these principles and concepts to work for the benefit of all of us. Let's not waste another day. Let's be about our Father's business.

———— ∞ ————

Chapter 4

Crowns for the Family Unit

The fact that, as parents, we should pray for our children and guide them in the things of God should be understood. However, the onslaught against families and the family unit over the last few decades has had a profound impact on even the most fundamental concepts of parenting.

More grandparents are raising their grandchildren than ever before. More parents are relinquishing their roles to raise their children in the nurture and admonition of the Lord.

Ephesians 6:4:

> *And you, fathers, do not provoke your children to wrath, but bring them up in the training and admonition of the Lord.*

Or as The Passion Translation says:

> *Fathers, don't exasperate your children, but raise them up with loving discipline and counsel that brings the revelation of our Lord. (TPT)*

With the revelation of the crowns, we now understand that these challenges are demonstrations of crowns that have been lost.

For the parents who have abandoned or abdicated the role of parenting to the grandparents or the foster system, they have had their Crown of Godly Parenting stolen from them. They are missing the Crown of Nurture and other crowns related to loving their offspring.

These parents have forced grandparents or foster parents to take on the responsibilities they have abandoned. That is extremely selfish on the part of the parents, for grandparents should be able to enjoy their grandchildren in their role as grandparents, not as parents. Parents, you are stealing from your parents when you do this.

For some abdicating parents, the enemy has ensnared you in a vice or lifestyle related to the false crowns we discuss in this book. Own your sins, get the false, ungodly crowns removed, and gain the right crowns so you can resume your role as the primary caregiver in your children's lives.

> *Parents: don't continue
> to be broken people,
> reproducing broken children.
> Become whole!*

Assume your role. It's one of the rewards for the fun you had creating them.

Grandparents who have become (for the second time), the primary caregivers, I commend you and encourage you to love those children to Jesus and help them learn to become responsible young men and women who don't shirk responsibility and who become self-governing within a relationship with the Father. Receive the crowns necessary for you to raise those children effectively.

Parents who have not abdicated their role as primary caregivers step into the Court of Crowns and receive every crown needed to fulfill their role.

In this book, we will show you some ways to intercede for your children and seven of the most impactful false crowns the enemy aims to place on your life and the lives of your children. You need to know what to pay attention to, so your family stays intact in your walk with the Father.

Where you may have lost or forfeited crowns or had them stolen from your life, we will show you how to reclaim them.

Parents, be aware that the enemy will attempt to send people across your path, your spouse's path, and your children's path whose job is to steal crowns. Be aware of that strategy. These spoilers can do significant damage.

To single parents, I commend you for taking on the tough job of raising your children without the shared help of the other parent. Heaven has grace and crowns that can help you. Step into the Court of Crowns and check your Book of Crowns to see what crowns are available to you for the tasks at hand.

If you are a foster parent, I commend you as well. Crowns are also available to you. Wisdom and grace are also needed. Again, find out what is available in the Court of Crowns for you and your parents honorably before the Lord.

If you are a minor child or still living with your parents as an adult, check with the Court of Crowns for the crowns Heaven has for you. Honoring your parents is necessary. If you honor them, you can benefit from having them in your life. Always honor them. Adult children don't mooch off your parents. They don't have to provide for you at this stage in your life. It is not an eternal obligation of a parent to be responsible for adult children. Be accountable for yourself. Always have an exit strategy. If you have the means, pay room and board. You would have to do that if they weren't around. If you don't have a job, be diligent in finding one or creating one. Let your parents enjoy an empty nest. They have earned it. They raised you, didn't they?

─────── ∞ ───────

Chapter 5
Basic Categories of Wickedness

In my book, *Embracing Your Crown of Authority*, I discussed the seven false crowns coming from the red dragon of Revelation 12:3:

> *Then, I witnessed in Heaven another significant event. I saw a large red dragon with seven heads and ten horns, with **seven crowns on his heads**. (Emphasis mine) (NLT)*

These appear to be categories of wickedness that we deal with regularly and are the basis for many of the assaults on the family unit. The seven false crowns are:

- The False Crown of Deception
- The False Crown of Loathing
- The False Crown of Fear
- The False Crown of Devouring
- The False Crown of Magic
- The False Crown of Secrets
- The False Crown of Antichrist

As we understand the earmarks of these false crowns, you will see how many families have embraced and wear them in their daily lives. The aim of many in embracing these false crowns may not be power or prestige, but the result of these false crowns working against the family unit is to destroy it and the lives involved.

For some, it is quite evident that, in their pursuit of power, they have sought false crowns that would enable a rise to prominence and/or influence. However, you can have prominence but no influence, just as you can have influence without prominence. Most seem to crave prominence and desire influence, but influence doesn't necessarily mean they have a significant impact. Often, when someone is causing harm to a situation, our court work can be directed to removing their influence or impact, or both. These issues are more likely to affect parents than children, at least until the children are older and want to establish their footing in the world.

As intercessors, we often forget that when someone lives outside God's will, they have allowed the wrong substance to fill their Crown of Authority. Many are outside God's plan for their lives, especially if they have adopted ideals that are contrary to the welfare of those under their influence. We must remember that many are deceived and are under the influence of one or more of these false crowns.

Our responsibility is to help them find freedom and begin living under the right crowns for their lives. We must also remember that unless we love someone, we do not have the right to pray for them because we will pray incorrectly concerning them. We must operate from our spirit, not from our soul or emotional realm. The Father can give you love for those in your life so that you can pray and intercede appropriately for them.

Usually, love within a family is not an issue. Still, when you have blended families due to divorces and remarriages, it can sometimes be a challenge for some to have the necessary love for those they did not give birth to. The adults need a Crown of Godly Parenting.

As we unveil these false crowns, you will begin to recognize when they are at work in someone's life. That will help you have more targeted intercession on their behalf. The more specific we can be in our prayers or court work, the more impactful the results. Remember, we want to see every inferior crown replaced with a Superior Crown of Heaven.

——— ∞ ———

Chapter 6

The False Crown of Deception

The first false crown we will learn about is the Crown of Deception (also known as the Crown of Deceit). You will recognize that this crown is a common feature in many people's lives. Some people you know wear this crown, but the great news is that we can be free.

The red dragon gives these false to the sons...those who should be seeking after truth. If a son does not govern the whispers of the enemy in his ears, those whispers become accusations, which become offenses and will divide that person from the truth about a person.

To explain this to small children, help them understand a whisper could be, "Mommy doesn't love me," or "Bobby is mean." If they think about those whispers too long, they may become accusations. The Bible says in 2 Corinthians 2:11:

> *The agenda of any accusation is to **divide** and **dominate**. (MIRROR) (Emphasis mine)*

Deception comes in many forms, but the primary way is through whispers. If someone takes offense, they open the door to deception and wrong actions.

If we refuse to acknowledge the truth in <u>any</u> area, we can disqualify ourselves from recognizing the truth in other areas.

This is a prized crown that the enemy loves to put on the heads of the sons. Think of it as a game. In this Crown of Deception, there is a stone of self-righteousness. All the "selves" are embedded in this inferior crown: self-righteousness, self-hatred, and self-loathing coexist, along with self-idolization, self-importance, and self-justification, which is lethal.

The Crown of Deception appears to be a good crown, but it is not.

As sons, we must discern. When this crown is put upon the head of a son, the wrong master is in control. He often experiences "delusions of grandeur" and thinks he is more right than anyone else. This form of self-righteousness is wicked; it will do anything to "stay right." If you haven't already, you will be presented with people who have this inferior crown.

Only the Superior Crowns of Heaven can trump this crown, as it is a delusion of grandeur. Many will not want to relinquish this crown until they're honest with themselves and the Father.

Many prophets wear this inferior crown. They begin to think they are infallible and are certainly not to be questioned. If they can't be challenged or their words recorded, separate from them.

The basis of this crown is pride.

This is a crown a narcissist wears, as well as the deeply wounded person. You will often find it on the heads of those who walk in orphanhood—not knowing their Heavenly Father.

How do we guard against this?

We must walk in humility, not grandiosity.

Galatians 6:1:

> *Brethren, if a man is overtaken in any trespass, you who are spiritual **restore such a one in a spirit of gentleness, considering yourself** lest you also be tempted. (Emphasis mine)*

Those who wear this crown lack humility. The sons must walk in humility, as peace will be their umpire. Those who wear this crown have no peace. Everyone who wears this crown *is looking for acceptance*. How many people have we seen who are broken and looking for acceptance?

The desire for acceptance makes people susceptible to this crown.

Many generations bowed their knee to this dragon of pride and were given great understanding—false wisdom. Again...

When working with someone, often, if they are wearing an inferior crown, they can't see that they need it to be removed. Self-striving is involved. Remember, all the "selves" are embodied in this crown.

A key to humility is a contrite heart. Contriteness is to show remorse. Many who follow LifeSpring have family members who wear this Crown of Deception. Repentance work is key. The Superior Crown of Love is the exchange. As a parent, be sure to place the Superior Crown of Love upon your spouse or children.

Some scriptures talk about contriteness:

Psalm 34:18:

> *The Lord is near to those who have a broken heart and saves **(deliver)** such as have a contrite spirit. (Emphasis mine)*

Isaiah 57:15:

> *The high and lofty one who lives in eternity, the Holy One, says this: 'I live in the high and holy place with those whose spirits are contrite and humble. I restore the crushed spirit of the humble and revive the courage of those with repentant hearts.' (NLT)*

And then Isaiah 66:2:

> *My hands have made both heaven and earth; they and everything in them are mine. I, the LORD, have spoken! 'I will bless those who have humble and contrite hearts, who tremble at my word.' (NLT)*

If someone in the family is already wearing this false crown, you must address the pride. If they don't have the fear of the Lord operating in their life, they will gladly wear this false crown. The enemy would love to give you and those in your family these crowns.

To bring people to freedom who have found themselves wearing this crown, remember that:

- Humility on your part and the other party's part is key.

- We must let peace be our umpire, not the accolades of those around us.
- We must be willing to repent and forgive.
- We must have remorse for our improper behavior. Having a fear of the Lord in our lives makes us much more willing to do this.
- We must own our pride. Many people have pride as a significant issue. We are what we are by the Father's grace upon our lives.

Identifying the False Crown of Deception

- They are self-righteous.
- All the "selves" manifest in this crown: self-righteousness, self-hatred, and self-loathing are together, along with self-idolization, self-importance, and self-justification.
- They are always striving.
- Nothing negative that happens is their fault
- They present themselves as good when underneath, they have evil intent.
- They often have delusions of grandeur.
- They may consider themselves prophetic.
- They think they are infallible.
- Do they have narcissistic tendencies?
- Are they prideful?
- They are deeply broken underneath.
- They have no humility.

- They have a strong desire for acceptance.
- They have no fear of God.

How Do These Characteristics Affect Families

These characteristics describe a deeply wounded, spiritually misaligned individual, someone who has not submitted their inner world to the Lord, yet may be operating from a religious or authoritative posture. When these traits manifest within a family, the impact can be devastating, affecting identity, communication, spiritual development, emotional safety, and the generational legacy.

Let's walk through **how each of these traits negatively impacts a family**, especially when operating through a parent, spouse, or spiritual leader in the home.

1. They are self-righteous.

Impact: This creates an atmosphere of **judgment and control**. Children and spouses feel they must "measure up" or walk on eggshells. Grace is absent, and performance is demanded. This crushes vulnerability and builds walls instead of connection.

2. All the "selves" manifest: self-righteousness, self-hatred, self-loathing, self-idolization, self-importance, self-justification.

Impact: This creates **emotional chaos and confusion**. The person may swing between superiority and insecurity, making their family feel responsible for their moods. Their identity is unstable, so they project instability onto others, especially children, who may internalize blame or become overly self-critical.

---

3. They are always striving.

Impact: The home becomes a place of **hustle, not rest**. There's little joy or peace because success, appearance, or control is constantly pursued. Family members may feel like tools in a personal mission rather than treasured individuals.

---

4. They never take responsibility for anything negative.

Impact: This fosters **blame-shifting and emotional abuse**. Others are always the scapegoats. This erodes trust and teaches children to suppress their voice, or worse, adopt the same pattern. Emotional honesty is punished, and accountability is non-existent.

---

5. They appear good, but harbor evil intent underneath.

Impact: This is **deceptive and dangerous**. It creates a double-life culture where image is everything and truth is buried. Family members sense that something is "off," but they can't speak up without being shamed or gaslit.[6] It breeds spiritual trauma.

---

6. They often have delusions of grandeur.

Impact: They may believe the family revolves around their "calling" or greatness. This elevates their personal goals above the needs of others. Children grow up **feeling invisible**, spouses feel like accessories to an agenda, and the family becomes spiritually imbalanced.

---

7. They may consider themselves prophetic.

Impact: If unsubmitted to wise counsel, this becomes **spiritual manipulation**. They may use "God told me" language to control decisions or silence

---

[6] **Gaslighting** is a form of psychological manipulation where someone makes another person question their own reality, memory, or perceptions. The manipulator systematically denies, contradicts, or distorts the victim's experiences to make them doubt their sanity or judgment.

disagreement. True prophetic flow brings freedom; this brings **fear and confusion**.

8. They think they are infallible.

Impact: This breeds a **culture of fear and silence**. Admitting a mistake is impossible for them, so others stop trying to share the truth. Children may either rebel or internalize the idea that mistakes make them unlovable.

9. Do they have narcissistic[7] tendencies?

Impact: Narcissism **distorts reality**. Everything becomes about their needs, their story, their reputation. Empathy is absent. Family members feel used, unseen, or emotionally violated. It often leads to long-term trauma and emotional detachment.

---

[7] **Narcissism** is a personality pattern characterized by an inflated sense of self-importance, a deep need for excessive attention and admiration, and a lack of empathy for others. People with narcissistic traits believe they are superior, special, or entitled to preferential treatment.

10. Are they prideful?

Impact: Pride blocks **intimacy and repair**. The person never admits they're wrong, never apologizes, and resists help. Family members are left isolated, unable to build trust or grow together. Emotional distance becomes the norm.

---

11. They are deeply broken underneath.

Impact: Without healing, this brokenness **seeps into every aspect of life**. It produces emotional volatility, projection, and unmet expectations. Until the root is addressed, the entire family lives under a cloud of tension and unpredictability.

---

12. They have no humility.

Impact: Humility is the soil where forgiveness and growth flourish. Without it, the home becomes **a stage, not a sanctuary**. Family members stop sharing, stop hoping, and may emotionally withdraw or spiritually disengage.

---

13. They have a strong desire for acceptance.

Impact: This can lead to **people-pleasing outside the home and controlling behavior within the home**. The individual seeks validation from the world while demanding perfection from their family. It creates a double standard and emotional confusion for children.

14. They have no fear of God.

Impact: This is the root cause of the issue. Without reverence for God, there's no accountability beyond self. The person becomes their own moral compass. They may use religious language, but there's no surrender. This opens the family to **spiritual deception, legalism, or licentiousness**, and cuts off the flow of Heaven's peace and presence.

Final Thought:

When these traits are active in a home, the spiritual ecosystem is **toxic and unstable**. Love is conditional, truth is suppressed, and the Spirit's presence is grieved. Long-term effects may include:

- **Spiritual abuse**
- Emotional estrangement
- Identity confusion in children
- Fear of authority
- Rejection of church or faith altogether

But **there is hope.** When the root is acknowledged, and repentance and healing are pursued, even deeply wounded families can be **restored, restructured, and renewed by God's grace.**

Removing a False Crown of Deception

1. Request entrance to the Court of Crowns.
2. Repent for embracing the Crown of Deception out of brokenness, arrogance, and pride.
3. Repent for every vestige of pride, arrogance, or brokenness in their life. Have them do the same.
4. Have them remove the false crown from your head.
5. Ask for the Crown of Humility, the Crown of Righteousness, and the Crown of Love to be placed on their heads.

Generational False Crowns

Sometimes, these false crowns are passed down from generation to generation. This is not limited to this false crown but could be the case with any false crowns. You want any false crown removed from your generational line.

Repent for those in your generational line who embraced the Crown of Deceit out of their brokenness, arrogance, and pride. Repent for any vestiges of pride, arrogance, or brokenness in your own life. Remove the inferior crown from your head and the crown on your generational line, and ask for the Crown of Humility in its place *and* a Crown of Righteousness.

Removal of a Generational False Crown

1. Repent for those in your generational line who embraced the Crown of Deceit out of their brokenness, arrogance, and pride.
2. Repent for any vestiges of pride, arrogance, or brokenness in your own life.
3. Remove the crown from your head and the crown on your generational line.
4. Ask for the Crown of Humility in its place, the Crown of Love, as well as the Crown of Righteousness.

When you see someone experiencing delusions of grandeur, look for this crown. Only the Superior Crowns trump this crown.

Remember, humility provides protection from these false crowns.

As Psalm 100:3 says:

Know that the LORD, He is God; **it is He who has made us, and not we ourselves;** *we are His people and the sheep of His pasture. (Emphasis mine)*

Personal Court Case
for the Removal of the False Crown of Deception

Father, we ask to enter the realms of Heaven through Jesus. I invite the Seven Spirits of God, and the angels. I ask to enter the Court of Mercy.

I request that You bring into this Court everyone in our generations, both mother and Father's side, as well as those related to us by blood, marriage, adoption, civil or religious covenants, all the way from Your hand in the Garden and all the way forward as far as it needs to go, as well as my cloud of witnesses. I request that the accuser of the brethren be brought into this Court.

Your Honor, I agree with the adversary that me and my generations have picked up this false Crown of Deception through pride, arrogance, lies, delusions of grandeur, false humility, and through all of the selves. I repent for every self-deception that we have accepted and traded with. I repent of self-idolization, and I repent for the times when we have been unteachable. I repent for self-promotion and self-striving instead of being led by Holy Spirit.

Father, I repent for deceiving others and for allowing this crown to rest upon their heads. I agree with the adversary that we have all been guilty of this. I repent for allowing the false mantle to fall, and for wearing it proudly.

I repent for hearing Your voice speaking to us to remove it, and instead, we agreed to hang onto it tightly. I repent for not taking the keys of the Kingdom of Heaven and closing these doors, realms, gates, and bridges.

I repent where You have allowed us to use the key of humility to close these doors forever, and instead, we rebelled. I repent for the dishonor we brought upon ourselves, others, and You, Lord, for wearing this Crown of Deception, agreeing with delusions of grandeur, and thinking of ourselves more highly than we ought to.

I repent for being distracted by this Crown of Deception and allowing its deception to bring us further and further and further away from the truth. I repent for being awestruck by the illusion of this crown.

I repent for the throne, which is the altar of worship, where we have worshipped ourselves, worshipped what we've accomplished, and even worshipped the pain in our thoughts and minds.

I ask that the angels come and take this altar, this throne, and the idols upon it, which are all of our self's. I repent for the use of this crown as well as every gray and black stone representing the self. I repent for where we have pride and present the crown, the throne, and the mantle to this court for judgment.

I ask that the angels bring every spirit associated with and assigned to this crown into the court for judgment. I now turn to our generations, and I forgive, bless, and release you for participating in this crown. I forgive them for perpetuating it through the generations and placing it upon the heads of others, and I repent for where I have placed it upon the heads of others. I ask for the blood of Jesus. I ask for the full destruction of the crown, the throne, and the mantle.

I request that the stain of this crown that was left upon the heads of the sons be removed by the blood of Jesus, and I ask that it become white as snow. I request the mantles be rent in two and torn as we bow in this court before the Just Judge of the Universe. We bow in humility. I say, 'Have mercy on us, Jesus.

I ask that You walk through the timeline in our generations. Please deliver to us Your Crown of Righteousness. I agree that we have strayed because of these false, inferior crowns. I ask that You take our hand and bring our generations back to the truth. I ask for mercy and Your righteous verdict on our behalf and those of our generations.

I ask that you please destroy and burn this inferior crown which is set on the seven-headed dragon, the dragon, its seven heads, its inferior crowns, thrones, mantles, scepters, altars, spiritual residue, essences, and debris, in Jesus' name.

I ask that the Superior Crowns of the Kingdom of Heaven be placed upon our heads, overturning the enormity of our sins.

I ask for renewed authorization for every crown restored to us and those to be restored today in Your court and the release of every mantle, throne, scepter, altar, anointing, and Glory.

I receive Your righteous verdict or further counsel, Your Honor.

[If further counsel is advised, follow these instructions. Once you have received a righteous verdict, begin the following segment:]

With our righteous verdict in hand, I speak to the earth. I speak to you that every one of our generations who stepped upon you, even those related to us by blood, marriage, adoption, civil or religious covenant.

Earth, I have received a righteous verdict from the Courts of Heaven this day. I bless you to hear the word of the Lord. I bless you to swallow up the iniquity and the egregious sins of self-deception and wearing these crowns. Swallow up every word and deed that was done upon you. Swallow the innocent bloodshed, sexual sins, moving of the boundary stones, worship of ourselves, idol worship, occultic worship, theft... every sin under the sun that Jesus died for. I charge you to swallow it up and bless you to your original design. I bless you to see the governing sons and to begin blessing us. Begin pouring out your riches of abundance of truth and life.

I request the blood of Jesus to cover every place this was done upon you or in you. I speak to the frequencies of the wind to blow away the evil, to the water to drown it, and to the fire to burn it. I speak to you to return to your original design as the Lord had created you. The Earth is the Lord's, and its fullness belongs to the Lord.

I speak peace. I thank the Just Judge. I thank You, Jesus, the author and the finisher of our faith, for the Crowns of Righteousness and the Crown of Love that trump this inferior crown.

As a governing son, I pick up these Superior Crowns, place them upon our heads, and ask you to help us rule. I commission the angels to render these righteous verdicts in the spirit and the natural. I commission the angels to put this on record.

As a son, I call in the treasure that has been lost from the north, the south, the east, and the west in every age, realm, dimension, and time to fill the capacity of this section.

Thank You, Just Judge, for honoring us and trusting us with the responsibility of wearing these Crowns of Love and Righteousness. Thank You for helping us occupy the territory you assigned us. I don't take this lightly and I ask for supernatural assistance and help daily to govern well as Your sons. In the name of Jesus.

I ask that all of this be done in time and out of time, and in every age, realm, and dimension, and that all of the spiritual debris, residue, and essences that were left behind by this inferior crown and the spirits that came with it be destroyed utterly. I thank You, Father, for what You did, Jesus, for giving us authority and dominion here.

Court Case
for the Removal of the False Crown of Deception
Off of Someone

Father, I ask to enter the realms of Heaven through Jesus on behalf of _____. I invite the Seven Spirits of God, the angels, and the accuser of the brethren. I ask to enter the Court of Mercy.

I request that You bring into this Court everyone in their generations, both their mother's and their father's side, as well as those related to them by blood, marriage, adoption, civil or religious covenants, all the way from Your hand in the Garden and all the way forward as far as it needs to go, as well as their cloud of witnesses.

Your Honor, I agree with the adversary that they and their generations have picked up this false Crown of Deception through pride, arrogance, lies, delusions of *grandeur, false humility, and through all of the selves. I repent for every self-deception that they have accepted and traded with. I repent for self-idolization, and I repent where they have been unteachable. I repent for self-promotion and self-striving instead of being led by Holy Spirit by them and their generations.*

Father, I repent for where they deceived others and for allowing this crown to rest upon their heads. I agree with the adversary that they have all been guilty of this. I repent for allowing the false mantle to fall and where they were glad to wear it proudly.

I repent for when they heard Your voice speaking to them to remove it, and instead, they agreed to hang onto it tightly. I repent for them not taking the keys of the Kingdom of Heaven and closing these doors, realms, gates, and bridges. I repent where you've allowed them to use the key of humility to close these doors forever, and instead, they rebelled. I repent for the dishonor they brought upon themselves, others, and you, Lord, for wearing this Crown of Deception, agreeing with delusions of grandeur, and thinking of themselves more highly than they ought to.

I repent for them being distracted by this Crown of Deception and allowing its deception to bring them further and further and further away from the truth. I repent for them being awestruck with the illusion of this crown.

I repent for the throne, which is the altar of worship, where they have worshipped themselves, worshipped what they have accomplished, and even worshipped the pain in their thoughts and minds.

I ask that the angels come and take this altar, this throne, and the idols upon it, which are all of their selfs. I repent for the use of this crown as well as every gray and black stone representing the selfs. I repent for where they have pride and I present the crown, the throne, and the mantle to this court for judgment.

I ask that the angels bring every spirit associated with and assigned to this crown into the court for judgment.

I turn now to their generations, and I forgive, bless, and release them for participating with this crown. I forgive them for perpetuating it through the generations and for placing it upon the heads of others and I repent for where they have placed it upon the heads of others as well. I ask for the blood of Jesus to cover this. I ask for the full destruction of the crown, the throne, and the mantle.

I request that the stain of this crown that was left upon the heads of the sons be removed by the blood of Jesus, and I ask that it become white as snow. I request the mantles be rent in two and torn as I bow in this court before the Just Judge of the Universe. I bow in humility. I say, 'Have mercy on them, Jesus. I ask that you walk through the timeline in their generations. Please deliver to them Your Crown of Righteousness. I agree that they have strayed because of these false, inferior crowns. I ask that you take their hand and bring their generations back to the truth. I ask for mercy and Your righteous verdict on their behalf and those of their generations.

I ask that you please destroy and burn this inferior crown which is set on the seven-headed dragon, the dragon, its seven heads, its inferior crowns, thrones, mantles, scepters, altars, spiritual residue, essences, and debris, in Jesus' name.

I ask for the Superior Crowns of the Kingdom of Heaven to be placed on our heads, overturning the egregiousness of our sins.

I ask for renewed authorization for every crown restored to us and those to be restored today in Your court and the release of every mantle, throne, scepter, altar, anointing, and Glory.

I receive Your righteous verdict or further counsel, Your Honor.

[If further counsel is advised, follow these instructions. Once you have received a righteous verdict, begin the following segment:]

With our righteous verdict in hand, I speak to the earth. I speak to you that every one of their generations who stepped upon you, even those related to them by blood, marriage, adoption, civil or religious covenant.

Earth, I have received a righteous verdict from the Courts of Heaven this day. I bless you to hear the word of the Lord. I bless you to swallow up the iniquity and the egregious sins of self-deception and wearing these crowns. Swallow up every word and deed that was done upon you. Swallow the innocent bloodshed, sexual sins, moving of the boundary stones, worship of themselves, idol worship, occultic worship, theft... every sin under the sun that Jesus died for. I charge you to swallow it up and bless you to your original design. I bless you to see the governing sons and to begin blessing them. Begin pouring out your riches of abundance of truth and life.

I request the blood of Jesus to cover every place this was done upon you or in you. I speak to the frequencies of the wind to blow away the evil, to the water to drown it, and to the fire to burn it. I speak to you to return to your original design as the Lord had created you. The Earth is the Lord's, and its fullness belongs to the Lord.

I speak peace. I thank the Just Judge. I thank You, Jesus, the author and the finisher of their faith, for the Crowns of Righteousness and the Crown of Love that trump this inferior crown.

As a governing son, I pick up these Superior Crowns, place them upon their heads, and ask you to help them rule.

I commission the angels to render these righteous verdicts in the spirit and the natural. I commission the angels to put this on record.

As a son, I call in the treasure that has been lost from the north, the south, the east, and the west in every age, realm, dimension, and time to fill the capacity of this section.

Thank you, Just Judge, for honoring them and trusting them with the responsibility of wearing these Crowns of Love and Righteousness. Thank you for helping them occupy the territory you assigned them. I don't take this lightly and ask for supernatural assistance and daily help to govern well as Your sons, in the name of Jesus.

I ask that all of this be done in time and out of time, and in every age, realm, and dimension, and that all of the spiritual debris, residue, and essences that were left behind by this inferior crown and the spirits that came with it be destroyed utterly. Thank You, Father, for what you did, Jesus, for giving us authority and dominion here.

Remember that the enemy is all about providing false solutions in your life. That is why this false crown is so deceptive. You may think you have a superior revelation or that you are exempt from certain things in your life that are against scripture—that certain rules don't apply to you.

A rejection of truth on any level can set you up to receive a false Crown of Deceit.

---- ∞ ----

Chapter 7
The False Crown of Loathing

The Crown of Loathing needs to be understood as it is a great crown of wickedness. To loathe something is to hate it deeply. It is the epitome of hatred. This crown *sits with injustice* and mandates the wickedness of injustice. This crown is the blackest of black, void of light, void of truth.

---
*Satan wears this crown
as he loathes God.*

Satan's hatred for the Father is so deep that he will do anything to hurt Him. To kill, steal, and destroy the sons deeply wounds the Father. This stems from loathing not only God but also the sons—His created ones.

Loathing has a stench to it, as does this crown. There is darkness, but an odd sense of belonging comes with this crown. To loathe something so deeply can give a sense of belonging that is false and in error.

The throne that accompanies this crown is a seat of wickedness and iniquity. Those who sit upon it sit not only in darkness in this life but in the next.

Hatred is vile. Hatred is devoid of love. This crown loathes love and anything that love brings. You will find that you may face opposition when working against this crown, as you are operating out of love, and it loathes anything that operates out of love.

Hatred consumes, and it consumes the innocent. There are aspects of loathing and hatred that consume even other dark entities. It is ferocious with a large appetite. The sons must grapple with hatred against God and man in their hearts.

Do not accept this crown or sit on its throne.

It will eat you alive and consume you.

It is utter darkness. That's why you must be careful with your heart.

> *The root of bitterness
> is the beginning of this crown
> being placed.*

The beginning of bitterness is offense, which generally starts when we do not govern the whisperings and innuendos. Let love be the ending. Desire the fruits of the Spirit.

Jesus died so that no one should wear this crown, and yet many do. With what Jesus did for us, we should never wear this crown. Some people who wear this feel accepted, but it is a false acceptance.

A significant aspect of this crown is the hatred. Many on the left politically wear this crown. They utterly loathe President Donald Trump, although they have likely never met him or tried to understand who he is and what he does. He is admittedly brash and no-nonsense, but in today's climate, America cannot afford someone without a backbone. Many with "Trump Derangement Syndrome" exhibit this false Crown of Loathing.

Some families are divided politically and will have to exercise diligence to ensure they give no place to this crown. If you cannot have a civil conversation with someone of a different opinion, it is a sign that you are wearing this crown. You may want to check your head apparel if you cannot or will not have a civil conversation. Ask yourself if you are wearing a false Crown of Loathing?

We need to look at a few scriptures and see if we need repentance work, such as 1 John 4:20-21:

> [20] *If someone says, 'I love God,' and **hates his brother**, he is a liar; for he who does not love his brother whom he has seen, how can he love God whom he has not seen?* [21] *And this commandment we have from Him: that he who loves God must love his brother also. (Emphasis mine)*

1 John 3:15:

> *Whoever **hates his brother** is a murderer, and you know that no murderer has eternal life abiding in him. (Emphasis mine)*

Proverbs 26:28:

> *A lying tongue **hates** those who are crushed by it, and a flattering mouth works ruin. (Emphasis mine)*

Identifying the False Crown of Loathing

- Are they filled with hate?
- Are they not concerned with justice?
- Do they work toward injustice?
- Do they hate any expression of love that is not self-serving?

- Is their hatred devoid of love and anything that love brings?
- Do they seek the destruction of those they disagree with?
- Are they ferocious at times?
- Do they act in such a way as to destroy those they don't like?
- Do they carry a root of bitterness?
- Do they carry offense?

How Do These Characteristics Affect Families

These characteristics describe a spiritually and emotionally hostile atmosphere—when present in the heart of a parent, spouse, or dominant family member, they don't just create dysfunction... they can **fracture the family at a soul-deep level**. They embody the opposite of the Kingdom culture of love, grace, justice, and reconciliation. Let's walk through how each one negatively impacts a family.

1. Are they filled with hate?

Impact: Hate is not just an emotion; it's a spiritual force that creates fear, insecurity, and emotional damage in the home. When hate is present, **love cannot flow freely.** Children may internalize this hate or mirror it in their relationships, leading to generational cycles of anger and rejection.

2. Are they not concerned with justice?

Impact: When fairness is absent, children feel unheard and powerless. Favoritism or unchecked wrongdoing often leads to **resentment and rebellion.** It also distorts their understanding of God's character, making Him seem unjust or indifferent.

3. Do they work toward injustice?

Impact: This is active harm. If a family leader intentionally manipulates, deceives, or abuses their position, it **undermines the core of trust.** The home becomes a place of harm instead of safety, and children often grow up with deep distrust toward all forms of authority.

4. Do they hate any expression of love that is not self-serving?

Impact: When love must always serve the person in control, it's not love—it's bondage. This form of emotional manipulation **teaches others to suppress affection, needs, and individuality.** Family members often feel used rather than cherished.

5. Is their hatred devoid of love and anything that love brings?

Impact: This reveals a **completely closed heart**—one that cannot give or receive real love. The family then becomes emotionally cold and disconnected. Affection feels unsafe. Vulnerability is punished. Over time, family members may emotionally dissociate as a means of survival.

6. Do they seek the destruction of those they disagree with?

Impact: This is a spirit of vengeance at work. If disagreement leads to punishment, sabotage, or humiliation, it creates a **climate of fear and silence.** Children and spouses will hide their thoughts, needs, and personalities, living in emotional exile.

7. Are they ferocious at times?

Impact: Explosive anger—even if it's not constant—keeps the household in a state of **fight or flight.** Everyone tiptoes around the "volcano," and peace becomes impossible. Children often suffer from anxiety, PTSD-like symptoms, or anger disorders of their own.

8. Do they act in such a way as to destroy those they don't like?

Impact: This is evidence of a **demonic stronghold**, not just woundedness. It invites a spirit of death and division. In families, this behavior severs relationships permanently, often resulting in **estrangement, spiritual trauma, and emotional exile.**

---

9. Do they carry a root of bitterness?

Impact: Bitterness defiles many (Hebrews 12:15). It poisons the spiritual water supply of the home. Conversations become laced with sarcasm, cynicism, or resentment. Bitterness also tends to reproduce itself—**children often grow bitter without knowing why.**

---

10. Do they carry offense?

Impact: Living offended blocks grace. The offended person becomes touchy, reactive, and unreconciled. In the home, this **shuts down communication, fuels silent treatment, and prevents healing** from conflict. It teaches children that unforgiveness is acceptable.

In Summary:

These characteristics create a **spiritually unsafe home**, marked by fear, tension, emotional manipulation, and deep wounding. Instead of nurturing identity and purpose, the family becomes a war zone of control, rejection, and punishment.

Long-term effects may include:

- Emotional detachment or breakdown
- Fear of closeness or intimacy
- A distorted view of love, justice, and God
- Repetition of abusive cycles in future generations

Removal of the Crown of Loathing

Do a self-check first.

1. Repent for where we have embraced the Crown of Loathing out of hatred and the root of bitterness.
2. Repent for embracing offense.
3. Repent for every vestige of hatred, disrespect, dishonor, and lying in your own life.
4. Remove the false crown from your head.
5. Request a cleansing of your realms from the vestiges of this false crown.
6. Ask for the Crown of Love for yourself.
7. Pray in the spirit for yourself.

Interceding for Those in the Family

1. Repent for where the person(s) has embraced the Crown of Loathing out of hatred and the root of bitterness.
2. Repent for them embracing offense.
3. Repent for every vestige of hatred, disrespect, dishonor, and lying in their life.
4. Remove the false crown from their head.
5. Request a cleansing of their realms from the vestiges of this false crown.
6. Ask for the Crown of Love to be placed upon them.
7. Pray in the spirit for them.

Personal Court Case
for the Removal of the Crown of Loathing

Father, I ask to step into the Court of Mercy to receive mercy in our time of need. I request the accuser of the brethren be brought in, as well as our generations, those related to us by blood, marriage, adoption, civil or religious covenant, all the way from Your hand in the garden and as far forward as it needs to go, as well as my cloud of witnesses.

I come to you, and I repent for embracing the Crown of Loathing out of hatred and the root of bitterness. I repent for embracing offense, and I repent for every vestige of hatred, disrespect, dishonor, and lying in our own lives.

I repent where I have ever loathed anyone or anything in our generations, I repent where I have allowed, agreed with, or perpetuated the spirit of antichrist, but also where I was or am anti-God, where I let this inferior crown bring an atheistic mentality. I repent for cooperating with that. I repent for our hatred of the Father and those who are His. I repent for engaging in the stench of these sins. I repent for sitting in league with injustice, promoting injustice, and being unjust. I repent for mandating the wickedness of injustice.

I repent for being void of truth. I repent for agreeing with, being a part of, and loving the sense of belonging by wearing this inferior crown. I repent for sitting on the throne of loathing with its seat of wickedness and iniquity. I repent for the great error of wearing this crown.

I repent for believing the false acceptance, the pride, and the belief that I do not have to love you or anyone else, only ourselves. Please forgive us. I repent for loathing love. I repent for not accepting your love and for not loving others or even ourselves.

Father, forgive us and our generations, those who were atheists, those who loathed the Word of God, the truth around it, and those who had bitterness in their hearts; I repent. I repent for the utter hatred of anything that presented itself from you or from others that were or carried the embodiment of Your love or what it would bring. I repent for having an appetite for loathing and for hating you, God and man.

I ask for the angels to go through time, on behalf of ourselves and our generations, to remove the crowns of loathing and destroy them.

I ask the angels to remove the Crowns of Loathing placed upon our family's heads, of those who don't trust or believe, for it came from an iniquitous generation. I ask that the throne be destroyed, the seat of wickedness be destroyed, and iniquity be forever vanquished, banished, and removed forevermore from us and our generations. I repent for being a part of consuming the innocent and taking innocence away from others because of wearing this inferior crown. I repent for being a part of others losing their Superior Crowns, where I removed them, or where their crowns became lost.

Jesus, I ask for your blood to cover us and for those crowns to be removed from our children, our grandchildren, our mothers, our fathers, our sisters, our brothers, our friends, and our neighbors. I speak that it must bow to the Superior Crown of King Jesus and the crowns I wear—The Crown of Sonship and the Crown of Love, in Jesus' name.

Righteous Judge, I ask for your verdict or further counsel.

[If further counsel is advised, follow these instructions. Once you have received a righteous verdict, begin the following segment:]

I speak to the earth that every one of our generations who stepped upon you, even those related to us by blood, marriage, adoption, civil or religious covenant.

Earth, I have received a righteous verdict from the Courts of Heaven this day. I bless you to hear the word of the Lord. I bless you to swallow up the iniquity and the egregious sins of self-deception and wearing these inferior crowns. Swallow up every word and deed that was done upon you. Swallow the innocent bloodshed, sexual sins, moving of the boundary stones, worship of ourselves, idol worship, occultic worship, theft... every sin under the sun that Jesus died for. I charge you to swallow it up and bless you to your original design. I bless you to see the governing sons and to begin blessing us. Begin pouring out your riches of abundance of truth and life.

I request the blood of Jesus to cover every place this was done upon you or in you. I speak to the frequencies of the wind to blow away the evil, to the water to drown it, and to the fire to burn it. I speak to you to return to your original design as the Lord had created you. The Earth is the Lord's, and its fullness belongs to the Lord.

I speak peace. I thank the Just Judge. I thank You, Jesus, the author and the finisher of our faith, for the Crowns of

Righteousness and the Crown of Love that trump this inferior crown.

As a governing son, I pick up these Superior Crowns, place them upon our heads, and ask you to help us rule. I commission the angels to render these righteous verdicts in the spirit and the natural. I commission the angels to put this on record.

Thank you, Just Judge, for honoring us and trusting us with the responsibility of wearing these Crowns of Love and Righteousness. Thank you for helping us occupy the territory you assigned us. I don't take this lightly and ask for supernatural assistance and help daily to govern well as Your sons, in the name of Jesus.

As a son, I call in the treasure that has been lost from the north, the south, the east, and the west in every age, realm, dimension, and time to fill the capacity of this section.

Thank you, Just Judge, for honoring us and trusting us with the responsibility of wearing these Crowns of Love and Righteousness. Thank you for helping us occupy the territory you assigned us. I don't take this lightly, and I ask for supernatural assistance and help daily to govern well as Your sons, in the name of Jesus.

I ask that all of this be done in time and out of time, and in every age, realm, and dimension, and that all of the spiritual debris, residue, and essences that were left behind by this inferior crown and the spirits that came with it be destroyed utterly. I thank You, Father, for what you did, Jesus, for giving us authority and dominion here.

Court Case for the Removal of the Crown of Loathing Off of Someone

Father, I ask to step into the Court of Mercy to receive mercy in our time of need. I am stepping in on behalf of _____.

I request the accuser of the brethren of this person be brought in as well as their generations, those related to them by blood, marriage, adoption, civil or religious covenant, all the way from Your hand in the garden and all the way forward as far as it needs to go, as well as their cloud of witnesses.

I come to you, and I repent for their embrace of the Crown of Loathing out of hatred and the root of bitterness. I repent on their behalf for embracing offense, and I repent for every vestige of hatred, disrespect, dishonor, and lying in their life.

I repent for where they have ever loathed anyone or anything in their generations. I repent where they have allowed, agreed with, or perpetuated the loathing and hatred, but also where those who are or were anti-God, where I let this inferior crown to bring a hateful mentality. I repent for cooperating with that.

I repent for our hatred of the Father and those who are His. I repent for engaging in the stench of these sins. I repent for sitting in league with injustice, promoting injustice, and being unjust. I repent for mandating the wickedness of injustice.

I repent for them and their generations who hated those of other races or classes.

I repent for being void of truth. I repent for agreeing with, being a part of, and loving the sense of belonging by wearing this inferior crown.

I repent for sitting on the throne of loathing with its seat of wickedness and iniquity. I repent for the great error of wearing this crown. I repent for believing the false acceptance, the pride, and the belief that I do not have to love you or anyone else, only ourselves. Please forgive us. I repent for loathing love. I repent for not accepting your love and for not loving others or even ourselves.

Father, forgive them and their generations, those who were haters, those who loathed the Word of God, the truth around it, and those who had bitterness in their hearts; I repent.

I repent for their utter hatred of anything that presented itself from you or from others that were or carried the embodiment of Your love or what it would bring. I repent for them having an appetite for loathing and for hating you, God and man.

I ask for the angels to go through time, on behalf of them and their generations, to remove the crowns of loathing and destroy them.

I ask the angels to remove the Crowns of Loathing placed upon their family's heads, of those who don't trust or believe, for it came from an iniquitous generation. I ask that the throne be destroyed, the seat of wickedness be destroyed, and iniquity be forever vanquished, banished, and removed forevermore from them and their generations.

I repent for where they or their generations were a part of consuming the innocent and taking innocence away from others because of wearing this inferior crown. I repent for being a part of others losing their Superior Crowns, where I removed them, or where their crowns became lost.

Jesus, I ask for your blood to cover them and for those crowns to be removed from their children, their grandchildren, their mothers, their fathers, their sisters, their brothers, their friends, and their neighbors.

I declare that this inferior Crown of Loathing must bow to the Superior Crown of King Jesus and the crowns I wear—The Crown of Sonship and the Crown of Love, in Jesus' name.

Righteous Judge, I ask for your verdict or further counsel.

[If further counsel is advised, follow these instructions. Once you have received a righteous verdict, begin the following segment:]

I speak to the earth that every one of their generations who stepped upon you, even those related to them by blood, marriage, adoption, civil or religious covenant.

Earth, I have received a righteous verdict from the Courts of Heaven this day. I bless you to hear the word of the Lord. I bless you to swallow up the iniquity and the egregious sins of self-deception and wearing these inferior crowns. Swallow up every word and deed that was done upon you. Swallow the innocent bloodshed, sexual sins, moving of the boundary stones, worship of ourselves, idol worship, occultic worship, theft... every sin under the sun that Jesus died for. I charge you to swallow it up and bless you to your original design. I bless you to see the governing sons and to begin blessing us. Begin pouring out your riches of abundance of truth and life.

I request the blood of Jesus to cover every place this was done upon you or in you. I speak to the frequencies of the wind to blow away the evil, to the water to drown it, and to the fire to burn it. I speak to you to return to your original design as the Lord had created you. The Earth is the Lord's, and its fullness belongs to the Lord.

I speak peace. I thank the Just Judge. I thank You, Jesus, the author and the finisher of our faith, for the Crowns of Righteousness and the Crown of Love that trump this inferior crown.

As a governing son, I pick up these Superior Crowns, place them upon our heads, and ask you to help us rule. I commission the angels to render these righteous verdicts in the spirit and the natural. I commission the angels to put this on record.

Thank you, Just Judge, for honoring us and trusting us with the responsibility of wearing these Crowns of Love and Righteousness. Thank you for helping us occupy the territory you assigned us. I don't take this lightly and ask for supernatural assistance and help daily, so that they may govern as Your sons, in the name of Jesus.

As a son, I call in the treasure that has been lost from the north, the south, the east, and the west in every age, realm, dimension, and time to fill the capacity of this section.

Thank you, Just Judge, for honoring us and trusting us and them with the responsibility of wearing these Crowns of Love and Righteousness. Thank you for helping us all to occupy the territory you assigned us. I don't take this lightly, and I ask for supernatural assistance and help daily to govern well as Your sons, in the name of Jesus.

I ask that all of this be done in time and out of time, in every age, realm, and dimension, and that all the spiritual debris, residue, and essences left behind by this inferior crown and the spirits that accompanied it be utterly destroyed. I thank You, Father, for what you did, Jesus, for giving us authority and dominion here.

———— ∞ ————

Chapter 8
The False Crown of Fear

This crown operates quite strongly in both believers and unbelievers alike. It is the Crown of Fear.

When this crown is placed on someone's head, many demonic entities come with it and are released into the person's life. Picture how they may come in from a back door. It is a release of the essence of each of them, because fear comes with a lot of other negative things.

When this Crown of Fear is placed upon a person, it will open a throne, and all these negative things will begin pouring out, encircling their head and trying to manifest around, in, and through their mind.

2 Timothy 1:7:

For God has not given us a spirit of fear, but of power and of love and of a sound mind.

The Apostle Paul said, "I have not given you a spirit of fear," which is a specific dark entity. However, with the spirit of fear comes the Crown of Fear, and the enemy distributes this crown to many. Wearing this crown distorts the mind and even affects the heart. This crown rules over many of the other inferior crowns, making it superior to them.

Many people have this crown thrust upon them through traumas. When you have trouble receiving from Heaven, there may be fear coming from the generations. You may have to remove the Crown of Fear from your head continually.

This Crown of Fear is a master manipulator. It creates a stronghold, and when this crown is put on the heads of the sons, it is as if it tries to become embedded in them. It doesn't just sit on the head; it digs into the person's head, piercing it as if the crown were inverted.

Of course, we don't want anything to do with this crown and its ability to distort our ability to receive and flow in revelation. As a governing son, that should make you mad.

When you see it operating in the lives of others, it should also anger you. It is encroaching on their minds. Many people are driven by fear.

Identifying the False Crown of Fear

- Are they consumed with fear?
- Do they live in terror?
- Do they always circle back to something to fear?
- Do they have a negative mindset?
- Do they exhibit distorted thinking?
- Is their physical heart having issues?
- Do they have trouble receiving from Heaven?
- Do they have trouble receiving or flowing in revelation?

How Do These Characteristics Affect Families

Fear, especially when deeply rooted and partnered with distorted thinking, can **permeate the spiritual and emotional climate of a family**. When a parent, spouse, or key family figure carries these traits, they unintentionally shape the home into a place of anxiety, spiritual blockage, and relational instability. Let's walk through the impact of each one:

1. Are they consumed with fear?

Impact: When fear is the dominant force in a parent or spouse, the home becomes a place of **hyper-vigilance and caution, rather than peace**. Children learn to second-guess everything, suppress risks, and avoid emotional openness. It blocks the ability to trust God and others, creating a spiritual ceiling that hinders forward movement.

2. Do they live in terror?

Impact: Living in terror is fear magnified. It often leads to irrational behavior, emotional volatility, or **paralysis in decision-making**. Families with a terror-driven leader may feel like they're constantly preparing for a storm that never comes. This can breed trauma in children, who internalize a sense that the world—and God—are unsafe.

3. Do they always circle back to something to fear?

Impact: This reveals a **fear stronghold**—a pattern that replaces peace with perpetual threat. It's like living with a spiritual smoke alarm that never stops beeping. This constant circling back prevents healing, disrupts rest, and creates confusion about God's trustworthiness.

4. Do they have a negative mindset?

Impact: Negativity is contagious. In a family, it colors how children view themselves, their future, and their faith. A negative parent may criticize more than affirm, worry more than pray, and see problems where others see possibilities. This cultivates **hopelessness and insecurity** in those under their influence.

5. Do they exhibit distorted thinking?

Impact: Distorted thinking—shaped by trauma, spiritual oppression, or past abuse—can lead to **false narratives** within the family. A parent might interpret questions as rebellion or honesty as a sign of dishonor. This creates emotional disconnection and misunderstanding, **shutting down vulnerability** in the household.

6. Is their physical heart having issues?

Impact: In the spirit, the heart is the seat of love, courage, and relational connection. Physical heart issues may reflect **spiritual blockages**, such as bitterness, grief, or unhealed trauma. When a family member's heart is under physical duress, it can be a sign to pray into emotional or spiritual **constriction in the home's atmosphere.**

7. Do they have trouble receiving from Heaven?

Impact: A parent or spouse who can't receive peace, provision, or identity from Heaven will try to get those things from the people around them, usually through control, manipulation, or emotional withdrawal. This places pressure on the family to provide something only God can give.

8. Do they have trouble receiving or flowing in revelation?

Impact: When a family leader can't hear from God, **spiritual confusion or stagnancy** can follow. The home may lack vision, divine insight, or prophetic guidance. Children may grow up without seeing true intimacy with God modeled and may confuse religion with relationship.

Summary: How Fear and Distortion Wound the Family

Fear creates **an atmosphere of control**, where freedom, joy, and spiritual growth are suppressed. It:

- Robs families of rest and trust
- Trains children to live in survival mode
- Blocks faith-filled decision making
- Hinders revelation and spiritual inheritance
- Passes generational patterns of anxiety, avoidance, and unbelief

Personal Court Case
for the Removal of the Crown of Fear

Father, I ask to step into Your Court of Mercy to receive mercy in our time of need. I ask that our generations be brought into this Court and those related to us by blood, marriage, adoption, civil or religious covenant, from Your hand in the garden and as far forward as far as it needs to go, as well as my cloud of witnesses.

Father, I present to you, ourselves and our generations, and every one of us who ever wore this inferior crown, who willingly took this Crown of Fear, who even distributed it to other people in our family and our generations, and even those outside of our generations where we instilled fear, we presented fear, where we were a part of fear, where we perpetuated fear throughout the generational line, or we've accepted it, bent our knee to it, or even relished in, or relished in it in others. Forgive us, Lord; we repent. I ask for the blood of Jesus to be applied to this.

I am requesting that this inferior crown be removed from me and our generational line, as it pierced our heads. As the angels remove this crown, even though it is not easily taken off, along with every binding and every structure that would keep it upon the heads of the sons, that crown be taken off and destroyed.

I ask that the Superior Crown of Love be placed upon our heads to heal any woundedness and begin to mend our minds and mend the places of woundedness.

I ask that the technology of the Crowns of Sonship that we wear and the new day would infiltrate and destroy the technology of the Crown of Fear and that the nanotechnology of Jesus—of His love (for He has not given us the spirit of fear, but of power) and that the power and the dominion of the Superior Crown crush and destroy the inferior Crown of Fear.

Father has not given us the spirit of fear but of love. That love is the Supreme Crown over this inferior crown, and as the Crown of a Sound Mind is placed upon our heads, that it heals every wound of the mind and that the poison that came with that inferior Crown of Fear be drawn up out of us as we are made new.

I commission the angels to clean up the spiritual debris, residue, and essences that the spirit of fear has left behind, and we receive the Crown of Superiority from Jesus, the Crown of Love, the Crown of Power, the dominion over this, and the Crown of a Sound Mind. Thank you, Lord.

I come out of agreement with every superiority of this inferior crown. I am not in agreement with it. Where we and our generations agreed and where we were lied to, and we believed that there was nothing we could do because we were so gripped by fear; that is a lie. I come out of agreement with the lie of this inferior Crown of Fear. I ask for the cancellation and annulment of these lies.

I commission the angels to capture every demonic spirit that came with the spirit of fear that came through the back door of this as it opened the door to other spirits.

I commission the angels to gather up these spirits and take them to be judged—those that infiltrated the mind and the heart, those that brought the lies and instilled fear.

Father, I ask in the Courts of Heaven that these inferior spirits be judged on behalf of the sons. I receive Your righteous verdicts on behalf of us and our generations. I ask that these inferior crowns be destroyed. Thank you for the Crown of a New Day—of your new for us. Thank you for the Superior Crown of the mind of Christ and the Crown of Love. Thank You, Jesus. I ask Father for the healing balm for the wounds. When this inferior Crown of Fear is placed on people's heads, it creates ugly wounds.

Further, I request the destruction of this throne, mantle, and crown by the name and blood of Jesus.

I come out of agreement with the master of this crown. Forgive us where we traded and agreed with it.

I ask that you please destroy and burn this inferior crown which is set on the seven-headed dragon, the dragon, its seven heads, its inferior crowns, thrones, mantles, scepters, altars, spiritual residue, essences, and debris, in Jesus' name.

I ask that the Superior Crowns of the Kingdom of Heaven be placed upon our heads, overturning the enormity of our sins.

I ask for renewed authorization for every crown restored to us and those to be restored today in Your court and the release of every mantle, throne, scepter, altar, anointing, and Glory.

Your Honor, we respectfully request your righteous verdict or further counsel.

[If further counsel is advised, follow these instructions. Once you have received a righteous verdict, begin the following segment:]

I speak to the earth that every one of our generations who stepped upon you, even those related to us by blood, marriage, adoption, civil or religious covenant.

Earth, I have received a righteous verdict from the Courts of Heaven this day. I bless you to hear the word of the Lord. I bless you to swallow up the iniquity and the egregious sins of self-deception and wearing these inferior crowns. Swallow up every word and deed that was done upon you. Swallow the innocent bloodshed, sexual sins, moving of the boundary stones, worship of ourselves, idol worship, occultic worship, theft... every *sin under the sun that Jesus died for. I charge you to swallow it up and bless you to your original design. I bless you to see the governing sons and to begin blessing us. Begin pouring out your riches of abundance of truth and life.*

I request the blood of Jesus to cover every place this was done upon you or in you. I speak to the frequencies of the wind to blow away the evil, to the water to drown it, and to the fire to burn it. I speak to you to return to your original design as the Lord had created you. The Earth is the Lord's, and its fullness belongs to the Lord.

I speak peace. I thank the Just Judge. I thank You, Jesus, the author and the finisher of our faith, for the Crowns of Righteousness and the Crown of Love that trump this inferior crown.

As a governing son, I pick up these Superior Crowns, place them upon our heads, and ask you to help us rule. I commission the angels to render these righteous verdicts in the spirit and the natural. I commission the angels to put this on record.

Thank you, Just Judge, for honoring us and trusting us with the responsibility of wearing this Crown of Love and Crown of Righteousness. Thank you for helping us occupy the territory you assigned us. I don't take this lightly; ask for supernatural assistance and help daily to govern well as Your sons in the name of Jesus.

As a son, I call in the treasure that has been lost from the north, the south, the east, and the west in every age, realm, dimension, and time to fill the capacity of this section.

I ask that all of this be done in time and out of time, and in every age, realm, and dimension, and that all of the spiritual debris, residue, and essences that were left behind by this inferior crown and the spirits that came with it be destroyed utterly. I thank You, Father, for what you did, Jesus, for giving us authority and dominion here.

Court Case
for the Removal of the Crown of Fear
Off of Someone

Father, I ask to step into Your Court of Mercy to receive mercy in our time of need on behalf of _____. I ask that their generations be brought into this Court and those related to them by blood, marriage, adoption, civil or religious covenant, from Your hand in the garden and as far forward as far as it needs to go, as well as their cloud of witnesses.

Father, I present to you, _____ and their generations, and every one of them who ever wore this inferior crown, who willingly took this Crown of Fear, who even distributed it to other people in their family and their generations, and even those outside of their generations where I they instilled fear, presented fear, where they were a part of fear, where they perpetuated fear throughout the generational line, or accepted it, bent their knee to it, or even relished in, or relished it in others. Forgive them, Lord; I repent on their behalf. I ask for the blood of Jesus to be applied to this.

I am requesting that this inferior crown be removed from them and their generational line as it pierced their heads. I ask that the angels remove this crown (even though it is not easily taken off), along with every binding and every structure that would keep it upon their heads. I ask that the Crown of Fear be taken off and destroyed.

I ask that the Superior Crown of Love be placed upon their heads to heal any woundedness and begin to mend their minds and mend the places of woundedness.

I ask that the technology of the Crowns of Sonship that they wear and the new day would infiltrate and destroy the technology of the Crown of Fear and that the nanotechnology of Jesus—of His love (for He has not given them the spirit of fear, but of power) and that the power and the dominion of the Superior Crown crush and destroy the inferior Crown of Fear.

Father has not given us the spirit of fear but of love. That love is the Supreme Crown over this inferior crown, and as the Crown of a Sound Mind is placed upon their heads, that it heals every wound of the mind and that the poison that came with that inferior Crown of Fear be drawn up out of them as they are made new.

I commission the angels to clean up the spiritual debris, residue, and essences that the spirit of fear has left behind, so they receive the Superior Crown from Jesus— the Crown of Love, and the Crown of Power—the dominion over this, and the Crown of a Sound Mind. Thank you, Lord.

I come out of agreement with every form of superiority of the inferior Crown of Fear. They are not in agreement with it, and I am not in agreement with it. Where they and their generations agreed and where they were lied to, and they believed that there was not anything they could do because they were so gripped by fear; that is a lie. I come out of agreement with the lie of this inferior Crown of Fear. I ask for the cancellation and annulment of these lies.

I commission the angels to capture every demonic spirit that came with the spirit of fear that came through the back door of this as it opened up the door to other spirits.

I commission the angels to gather up these spirits and take them to be judged—those that infiltrated the mind and the heart, those that brought the lies and instilled the fear.

Father, I ask in the Courts of Heaven that these inferior spirits be judged on behalf of the sons. I receive Your righteous verdicts on behalf of them and their generations. I ask that these inferior crowns be destroyed.

I thank you for the Crown of a New Day—of your new for us. Thank you for the Superior Crown of the mind of Christ and the Crown of Love. Thank You, Jesus.

I ask Father for the healing balm for the wounds, for when this inferior Crown of Fear is placed on people's heads, it creates ugly wounds.

Further, I request the destruction of this throne, mantle, and crown by the name and blood of Jesus.

I come out of agreement with the master of this crown. Forgive us where they traded and agreed with it.

I ask that you please destroy and burn this inferior crown which is set on the seven-headed dragon, the dragon, its seven heads, its inferior crowns, thrones, mantles, scepters, altars, spiritual residue, essences, and debris, in Jesus' name.

I ask that the Superior Crowns of the Kingdom of Heaven be placed upon our heads, overturning the enormity of our sins.

I ask for renewed authorization for every crown restored to us and those to be restored today in Your court, as well as the release of every mantle, throne, scepter, altar, anointing, and Glory.

Your Honor, I respectfully request Your righteous verdict or further guidance.

[If further counsel is advised, follow these instructions. Once you have received a righteous verdict, begin the following segment:]

I speak to the earth that every one of their generations who stepped upon you, even those related to them by blood, marriage, adoption, civil or religious covenant.

Earth, I have received a righteous verdict from the Courts of Heaven this day. I bless you to hear the word of the Lord. I bless you to swallow up the iniquity and the egregious sins of self-deception and wearing these inferior crowns. Swallow up every word and deed that was done upon you. Swallow the innocent bloodshed, sexual sins, moving of the boundary stones, worship of themselves, idol worship, occultic worship, theft... every sin under the sun that Jesus died for. I charge you to swallow it up and bless you to your original design. I bless you to see the governing sons and to begin blessing them. Begin pouring out your riches of abundance of truth and life.

I request the blood of Jesus to cover every place this was done upon you or in you. I speak to the frequencies of the wind to blow away the evil, to the water to drown it, and to the fire to burn it. I speak to you to return to your original design as the Lord had created you. The Earth is the Lord's, and its fullness belongs to the Lord.

I speak peace. I thank the Just Judge. I thank You, Jesus, the author and the finisher of our faith, for the Crowns of Righteousness and the Crown of Love that trump this inferior crown.

As a governing son, I pick up these Superior Crowns, place them upon our heads, and ask you to help them rule. I commission the angels to render these righteous verdicts in the spirit and the natural. I commission the angels to put this on record.

Thank you, Just Judge, for honoring me and trusting me and them with the responsibility of wearing these Crowns of Love and Crowns of Righteousness. Thank you for helping them occupy the territory you assigned them. I don't take this lightly; ask for supernatural assistance and help daily to govern well as Your sons in the name of Jesus.

As a son, I call in the treasure that has been lost from the north, the south, the east, and the west in every age, realm, dimension, and time to fill the capacity of this section.

I ask that all of this be done in time and out of time, and in every age, realm, and dimension, and that all of the spiritual debris, residue, and essences that were left behind by this inferior crown and the spirits that came with it be destroyed utterly. I thank You, Father, for what you did, Jesus, for giving us authority and dominion here.

∞

Chapter 9
The False Crown of Magic

This crown is unusually beautiful and alluring. It appeared as a crown with purple stones mounted on it. The stones were a beautiful purple color. The crown the stones were mounted on was also beautiful, dark, and larger than the other crowns. This was important because from the back of the crown to the front, the stones were all the same size except for the one in the very front. The others were all mounted on different points, except the center stone. The middle point at the front of the crown was higher and had a beautiful, long, elongated purple stone, whereas all other stones were shorter. The crown itself was suspended in mid-air, and the scenery around it was pitch-black.

The enemy doesn't trust anyone, so the larger stone embedded in this crown was the eye for him to see what they did for him. It's like back-and-forth messaging. Because he doesn't trust anyone, he sets up a monitoring system in each crown. It is wicked technology.

Although its beauty is enchanting, it is not a suitable crown. It seems to have good, but the good is contaminated by darkness and falsehood. This was a *Crown of Magic*. It is the crown on the fifth head of the dragon.

It is tantalizing, which makes this crown unique. It is a deception that comes with witchcraft. This crown is unique.

The deception here is that many believe some forms of witchcraft are good.

We saw this culturally a few years ago with the popularity of the Harry Potter series. Years before, we were socially inoculated by the television show *Bewitched*. Growing up, we were taught the false narrative of a good witch versus an evil witch in the movie *The Wizard of Oz*. We have been pre-conditioned to the lie that there is good witchcraft and evil witchcraft. NO! It is all bad!

The brides of Satan wear this crown. It has an allure. It lures people in. It is filled with a lust for power. Many online games play on this theme. It has an elevation. This crown suspends those who wear it. They are in a realm of darkness that looks like light to them.

It feels like power. It entices their senses, and it is full of greed.

It is the most dishonoring of crowns as dishonor alights upon the heads of those who wear it, for they have indeed dishonored the Lord.

This crown has elements of truth that pull people in.

> *When a lie is embedded in the truth, it makes it all a lie.*

The spirit of whoring is with this crown. It has an insatiable appetite and is handcrafted in the depths of hell.

> *Many of these crowns come through the assignments on the generational line, where there has been a lot of witchcraft.*

We must remove these crowns from their generational line that came through bloodline iniquity and sin. Then, commission the angels to go and *blight* these crowns from the generational line. It is a blight in the bloodline from which these crowns originate. To blight something is essentially to smite it from the generational lines. Many lingering human spirits are attached to the generational line because of this crown.

When you remove the crowns through repentance, you remove the lingering human spirits who wear them. There will be a fight about it. They're not going to want to give them up. They have been empowered by these crowns operating on and through the generational line. However, they will be removed.

Know that blight is something that destroys or impairs. When that crown is on the bloodline, it seeks to destroy. Remember, light dispels the darkness.

This crown also has a throne that needs to be dismantled. It is very much like an altar.

Identifying the False Crown of Magic

- Have they embraced Harry Potter and other forms of witchcraft that they have no problem with?
- Is greed a problem with them?
- Do they have sexual issues?
- Do they have problems with lingering human spirits?
- Are they distrustful?
- Do they have an insatiable appetite for things?

How Do These Characteristics Affect Families

These characteristics open specific spiritual doors that can profoundly damage the health, unity, and purpose of a family. Each one—when left unaddressed—invites **confusion, chaos, compromise, or even spiritual bondage** into the household. Let's walk through how each trait can **negatively impact a family**, especially when present in a parent or spiritual authority within the home.

---

1. Have they embraced Harry Potter or other forms of witchcraft without conviction?

Impact: Engaging with witchcraft—no matter how "entertaining" it seems—invites **spiritual contamination**. It desensitizes hearts to the reality of the demonic and **normalizes rebellion, manipulation, and counterfeit power**. When embraced by a parent or allowed in the home, it opens **gateways for deception and confusion**. Children may struggle to discern between the holy and the profane, and a spirit of rebellion can take root subtly.

"For rebellion is as the sin of witchcraft..." (1 Samuel 15:23)

2. Is greed a problem with them?

Impact: Greed cultivates **self-centeredness** and elevates materialism over relationships and righteousness. In the home, this can lead to:

- Emotional neglect (valuing money over people)
- Competition between siblings or comparisons based on material gain
- Spiritual barrenness, as the pursuit of more replaces contentment in Christ

Greed also invites **Mammon's influence**, making the family vulnerable to anxiety, comparison, and division.

---

3. Do they have sexual issues?

Impact: Sexual sin—especially in secret—introduces **shame, confusion, and spiritual pollution**. It can manifest in the family as:

- Tension, mistrust, or emotional coldness
- Inappropriate exposure for children (direct or indirect)
- A spirit of perversion or lust affecting the atmosphere
- Marital breakdown, secrecy, or emotional abandonment

Even when hidden, sexual compromise **grieves the Spirit** and causes division in the soul ties within the family structure.

---

4. Do they have problems with lingering human spirits?

Impact: Lingering human spirits—those who haven't fully crossed over or are tied to trauma, death, or unrepentant covenants—can **haunt family spaces, confuse children, and disturb the spiritual clarity of the home.**

They often bring:

- Fear-based dreams or night terrors
- Sudden shifts in emotional behavior, especially in children
- Unexplained confusion, spiritual heaviness, or resistance to worship/prayer

Their presence indicates **unfinished spiritual business** and can block Heaven's flow of peace and presence.

---

5. Are they distrustful?

Impact: Distrust erodes connection. A distrustful leader in the home will often:

- Control rather than guide

- Assume the worst in others' motives
- Withhold affirmation or affection
- Create an environment where children or spouses **don't feel safe to be honest**

It builds walls instead of bridges, turning the home into a place of fear and competition rather than warmth and belonging.

---

6. Do they have an insatiable appetite for things?

Impact: This reflects a spirit of **lust or gluttony—not just for sex or food, but for power, affirmation, novelty, and possession.** It results in:

- Discontentment and constant striving
- Neglect of spiritual life and emotional intimacy
- Modeling idolatry to children, who may grow up with warped priorities

This "more is never enough" mindset replaces God's sufficiency with **endless consumption**, which breeds restlessness and identity confusion in the family.

Summary: The Collective Impact on the Family

When these traits are active, the home becomes spiritually fragmented. The fruit often includes:

- **Emotional disconnection**
- **Spiritual warfare** (especially in children)

- Cycles of addiction or shame
- Unspoken wounds or fear-based obedience
- Generational patterns of rebellion, secrecy, and division

Personal Court Case
for the Removal of the Crown of Magic

Father, I ask to step into Your Court of Mercy, through Jesus, on behalf of me and my generations. I ask that the accuser of the brethren be brought in as well as our generational line, from both sides of the family, and those who are with us by blood, marriage, adoption, civil or religious covenant, from Your hand in the garden and all the way forward as far as it needs to go, as well as my cloud of witnesses.

Your Honor, I agree with the adversary that we were deceived by magic and everything it encompasses.

I repent for magic, for the use of it, for the places in the generations that yielded to it, utilized it, for those who took it up, who felt empowered by it, who were deceived because of it, and for those who elevated themselves in believing the lie.

I repent for those in the generations who practiced magic but also deceived others with bits of truth to pull them into the lie. I repent on their behalf.

I repent on behalf of everyone who believed the lie, succumbed to it, and then projected it, and perpetuated it through the generational line.

I repent for agreeing with the spirit of whoring, for trading with it, for seducing because of it, and for allowing it.

I repent for the garments they wore. I ask that they be removed and destroyed now.

I repent, sir, all the way back to Your hand in the garden and all the way forward as far as it needs to go. Father, I repent for taking this inferior crown and for the use of this crown. Where they saw it as useful, yet it was a lie.

I repent where I put this inferior crown on other people's heads and our own.

On behalf of the lingering human spirits who are or who are not a part of our bloodline, as well as our generations who are now assigned to the bloodline because of taking up these inferior crowns. I repent on their behalf for every sin under the sun, which is egregious, which dishonored and brought dishonor to the Lord because of taking up and wearing these inferior crowns.

I commission the angels to go through the timelines, ages, and dimensions for every person who wore this inferior crown, and I commission you to take it off their heads as we stand before the Lord in repentance for them. I forgive, bless, and release them.

I ask the angels to open up the silver channel, take the demonic guard and the bosses who were assigned to these LHSs, to Jesus' feet for judgment. To every lingering human spirit in the generational line, you will go and see Jesus today. You are not staying.

I forgive you, bless you, and release you for what you were doing in and through the bloodline. You are removed this day by the hand of God because of repentance, which we are allowed to do. He forgave us, and I forgive you.

When you see Jesus, I suggest you ask Him for mercy. Angels, I commission you to destroy every inferior crown of witchcraft in the name of Jesus.

I ask for a Crown of Truth to be given to our generational line—the utter and distinct truth, the Superior Crown that causes all other inferior crowns to be dismantled and destroyed, as their knee must bow, in the name of Jesus.

I ask that the thrones and mantles be found, dismantled, and destroyed in every place throughout the generational line.

Where our generations set this up as a type of altar, I ask that it be destroyed, and that every attendant of every altar be captured and dealt with according to the will of the Father, and that the idol of witchcraft, as well as this Crown of Magic, be judged in the courts today.

I commission the angels to take every spirit or entity who has been assigned or associated with this throne, inferior crown, mantle, and scepter to be taken to court for judgment. I commission the angels to destroy the thrones forever, and that the altar of the Lord be established in their place, in and through the bloodline. I request that angels be assigned there to worship and that the Crown of Truth be established as it sits upon the altar of the Lord.

I request that every false scepter that came with this inferior crown and this throne, which was considered to be a wand, also be taken from the generational bloodline and be utterly destroyed, annulled, and removed. I ask that its frequency be dismantled and destroyed in the name of Jesus.

I request the realm of the inferior hovering crown, the realm from which it came, be closed, and that there be a closed, sealed door in and upon the line of the generations forevermore with no ability to reopen.

I request that the center stone of this inferior crown, which is the eye, be utterly crushed, annulled, canceled, destroyed, and blinded forever in, through, and upon the generational line.

I ask for the amendment of "As if it Never Were."

I ask that you please destroy and burn this inferior crown which is set on the seven-headed dragon, the dragon, its seven heads, its inferior crowns, thrones, mantles, scepters, altars, spiritual residue, essences, and debris, in Jesus' name.

I ask that the Superior Crowns of the Kingdom of Heaven be placed upon our heads, overturning the enormity of our sins.

I ask for renewed authorization for every crown restored to us, and those to be restored today in Your court, and the release of every mantle, throne, scepter, altar, anointing, and Glory.

I ask for our righteous verdicts or further counsel.

[If further counsel is advised, follow these instructions. Once you have received a righteous verdict, begin the following segment:]

I speak to the earth, water, air, and fire. I have received a righteous verdict, and since the world and the fullness of it belong to the Lord, I charge you to swallow up, drown, blow away and burn all evil words, deeds, lies, witchcraft, innocent bloodshed, sexual sins, occultic cauldrons, evil rooms, evil technologies, spells, hex's, vexes, incantations, voodoo, dark art, manipulation, monitoring, astral projections, evil projections, counterfeit intelligence, and any and all other darkness or evil done upon the earth, through the air, to the water and using fire.

I bless you to the fullness of your original design and charge you to bless us as the Lord walks through time, restoring it and you to their fullness. I do this in the name and by the blood of Jesus, and as a governing son.

As a son, I call in the treasure that has been lost from the north, the south, the east, and the west in every age, realm, dimension, and time to fill the capacity of this section.

I ask that all of this be done in time and out of time, and in every age, realm, and dimension, and that all of the spiritual debris, residue, and essences left behind by this inferior crown and the spirits that came with it be destroyed utterly. I thank You, Father, for what you did, Jesus, for giving us authority and dominion here.

Court Case
for the Removal of the Crown of Magic
Off of Someone

Father, I ask to step into Your Court of Mercy, through Jesus, on behalf of _____ and their generations. I ask that the accuser of the brethren be brought in as well as their generational line, from both sides of the family, and those who are with them by blood, marriage, adoption, civil or religious covenant, from

Your hand in the garden and as far forward as it needs to go, as well as their cloud of witnesses.

Your Honor, I agree with the adversary that they were deceived by magic and everything it encompasses.

I repent for magic, for the use of it, for the places in their generations that yielded to it, utilized it, for those who took it up, who felt empowered by it, who were deceived because of it, and for those who elevated themselves in believing the lie.

I repent for those in their generations who practiced magic but also deceived others with bits of truth to pull them into the lie. I repent on their behalf.

I repent on behalf of everyone in their generations who believed the lie, succumbed to it, and then projected it, and perpetuated it through the generational line.

I repent for agreeing with the spirit of whoring, for trading with it, for seducing because of it, and for allowing it.

I repent for the garments they wore. I ask that they be removed and destroyed now.

I repent, sir, all the way back to Your hand in the garden and all the way forward as far as it needs to go. Father, I repent for taking this inferior crown and for the use of this crown. Where they saw it as useful, yet it was a lie.

I repent where they put this inferior crown on other people's heads and their own.

On behalf of the lingering human spirits who are or who are not a part of our bloodline, as well as their generations who are now assigned to the bloodline because of taking up these inferior crowns. I repent on their behalf for every sin under the sun, which is egregious, which dishonored and brought dishonor to the Lord because of taking up and wearing these inferior crowns.

I commission the angels to go through the timelines, ages, and dimensions for every person who wore this inferior crown, and I commission you to take it off their heads as we stand before the Lord in repentance for them. I forgive, bless, and release them.

I ask the angels to open up the silver channel, take the demonic guard and the bosses who were assigned to these LHSs, to Jesus' feet for judgment. To every lingering human spirit in the generational line, you will go and see Jesus today. You are not staying.

I forgive you, bless you, and release you for what you were doing in and through the bloodline. You are removed this day by the hand of God because of repentance, which we are allowed to do. He forgave us, and I forgive you.

When you see Jesus, I suggest you ask Him for mercy. Angels, I commission you to destroy every inferior crown of witchcraft in the name of Jesus.

I ask for a Crown of Truth to be given to our generational line—the utter and distinct truth, the Superior Crown that causes all other inferior crowns to be dismantled and destroyed, as their knee must bow, in the name of Jesus.

I ask that the thrones and mantles be found, dismantled, and destroyed in every place throughout the generational line.

Where their generations set this up as a type of altar, I ask that it be destroyed, and that every attendant of every altar be captured and dealt with according to the will of the Father, and that the idol of witchcraft, as well as this Crown of Magic, be judged in the courts today.

I commission the angels to take every spirit or entity who has been assigned or associated with this throne, inferior crown, mantle, and scepter to be taken to court for judgment. I commission the angels to destroy the thrones forever, and that the altar of the Lord be established in their place, in and through the bloodline. I request that angels be assigned there to worship and that the Crown of Truth be established as it sits upon the altar of the Lord.

I request that every false scepter that came with this inferior crown and this throne, which was considered to be a wand, also be taken from the generational bloodline and be utterly destroyed, annulled, and removed. I ask that its frequency be dismantled and destroyed in the name of Jesus.

I request the realm of the inferior hovering crown, the realm from which it came, be closed, and that there be a closed, sealed door in and upon the line of the generations forevermore with no ability to reopen.

I request that the center stone of this inferior crown, which is the eye, be utterly crushed, annulled, canceled, destroyed, and blinded forever in, though, and upon the generational line.

I ask for the amendment of "As if it Never Were."

I ask that you please destroy and burn this inferior crown which is set on the seven-headed dragon, the dragon, its seven heads, its inferior crowns, thrones, mantles, scepters, altars, spiritual residue, essences, and debris, in Jesus' name.

I ask that the Superior Crowns of the Kingdom of Heaven be placed upon our heads, overturning the enormity of our sins.

I ask for renewed authorization for every crown restored to us, and those to be restored today in Your court, and the release of every mantle, throne, scepter, altar, anointing, and Glory.

I ask for our righteous verdicts or further counsel.

[If further counsel is advised, follow these instructions. Once you have received a righteous verdict, begin the following segment:]

I speak to the earth, water, air, and fire. I have received a righteous verdict, and since the world and the fullness of it belong to the Lord, I charge you to swallow up, drown, blow away and burn all evil words, deeds, lies, witchcraft, innocent bloodshed, sexual sins, occultic cauldrons, evil rooms, evil technologies, spells, hex's, vexes, incantations, voodoo, dark art, manipulation, monitoring, astral projections, evil projections, counterfeit intelligence, and any and all other darkness or evil done upon the earth, through the air, to the water and using fire.

I bless you to the fullness of your original design and charge you to bless us as the Lord walks through time, restoring it and you to their fullness. I do this in the name and by the blood of Jesus, and as a governing son.

As a son, I call in the treasure that has been lost from the north, the south, the east, and the west in every age, realm, dimension, and time to fill the capacity of this section.

I ask that all of this be done in time and out of time, and in every age, realm, and dimension, and that all of the spiritual debris, residue, and essences left behind by this inferior crown and the spirits that came with it be destroyed utterly. I thank You, Father, for what you did, Jesus, for giving us authority and dominion here.

———— ∞ ————

Chapter 10
The False Crown of Secrets

This inferior crown is unlike any other. It is quiet and stealthy. It silences the sons. It is bloodthirsty, and it screams of desire to pierce frequencies, and it walks with the spirit of death. Its inner workings are harlotry, divination, and mockery.

The sounds of intercession rub and excoriate the head of this dragon, which is why it seeks to silence the sons. The Pharisees wore this crown with their lofty robes. Violence comes from the mouth of this dragon who wears this crown.

This Crown of Secrets works in tandem with the Crown of Antichrist. A cloak hides this dragon's head.

This crown is the seat
of Freemasonry,
so it has a throne.
It is shrouded in secrecy.

Degree levels of Freemasonry also have crowns. It revels in its deception. In this crown is fantasy that cooperates with harlotry. Simply look at the titles of the various degrees of Freemasonry. It is almost as if they were creating this weird world with fantastical titles. This is the defilement of the imagination.

This crown not only seeks silence but also mocks the sons. Its mouth is full of corruption, indignity, and falsehood. It's stealthy in nature.

Every secret will be revealed. Secrets shroud, but the uncovering is unbearable. It is the Lord who uncovers that many times.

---

*It is this head of the dragon
that seeks to shame
and silence the sons.
Have no secrets within you.*

Recently, the pastor of a large church in the Dallas/Fort Worth area was forced to resign due to something that happened with an underage woman many years ago. His secret came out, silencing and shaming him.

The old saying, "Be sure your sin will find you out, has much truth in it."

---
*Remove and destroy
this crown from your heads.
It is unbecoming of a son.*

James 5:16:

> **Confess your trespasses to one another,** *and pray for one another, that you may be healed. The effective, fervent prayer of a righteous man avails much. (Emphasis mine)*

Regret is in this crown. You must crush this serpent under your feet.

Don't fall into its trap. *Govern* this crown, remove it, and destroy it. The sons bear the responsibility of secrets.

Deuteronomy 29:29:

> *The **secret things belong to the LORD** our God, but those things which are revealed belong to us and to our children forever, that we may do all the words of this law. (Emphasis mine)*

Psalms 25:14:

> *The secret of the LORD is with those who fear Him, and He will show them His covenant.*

Mark 4:22:

*For there **is nothing that is hidden that won't be disclosed,** and **there is no secret that won't be brought out into the light!*** (Emphasis mine)

Identifying the False Crown of Secrets

- Do they appear religious on the surface?
- Do they mock believers?
- Do they seek to silence believers?
- Do they shame people?
- Do they "kick back" at the thought of intercession?
- Are they violent when challenged?
- Are they involved in Freemasonry or other secret organizations?
- Will they disparage someone of a different mindset?
- Do they appear religious on the surface?

How Do These Characteristics Affect Families

These characteristics are the hallmarks of **religious deception wrapped in spiritual pride**—a counterfeit mantle of authority and "godliness" that, when present in the family context, does **deep emotional, spiritual, and relational damage.** It creates a home where the appearance of faith replaces the heart of faith, and where **control, fear, and shame** prevail over love, truth, and freedom. Let's explore how each one can negatively affect a family.

1. Do they appear religious on the surface?

Impact: This duplicity creates **spiritual confusion and emotional trauma**, especially in children. When a parent talks about God but lacks love, grace, or authenticity, it teaches the family:

- That faith is a performance
- That God is angry or impossible to please
- That truth can be twisted to justify control

It turns Jesus into a taskmaster rather than a Redeemer and **drives children away from an authentic relationship with God.**

2. Do they mock believers?

Impact: Mockery is the language of contempt. When someone mocks other believers, especially those who are Spirit-filled or devoted, it creates **a culture of dishonor.**

- It silences spiritual hunger in the home
- It causes children or spouses to feel ashamed of their sensitivity to God
- It cultivates cynicism and shuts down childlike faith

This is especially damaging when the mocker claims spiritual superiority or leadership in the home.

---

3. Do they seek to silence believers?

Impact: This behavior is rooted in control and intimidation. It prevents spiritual growth and:

- Suppresses the Holy Spirit's movement in the home
- Punishes vulnerability or spiritual expression (prayer, worship, dreams, etc.)
- Models fear of man more than fear of God

Family members often internalize the message: *"My voice doesn't matter. My spiritual experiences are wrong."*

---

4. Do they shame people?

Impact: Shame is a tool of spiritual abuse. Instead of correction leading to growth, shame leads to:

- **Identity distortion**: Children grow up thinking they're flawed, not just that they made a mistake
- **Fear-based obedience** rather than loving surrender
- Emotional withdrawal, silence, and performance-driven living

This kind of atmosphere creates a **false holiness** that appears disciplined but is spiritually dead inside.

5. Do they "kick back" at the thought of intercession?

Impact: Resistance to intercession shows a **hardness of heart and spiritual pride.** It stifles:

- The prophetic voice in the family
- God's strategy for healing, deliverance, or breakthrough
- Children or spouses who may carry intercessory callings

Their resistance often spiritually "locks" the home, preventing revelation, protection, and prophetic clarity from flowing.

6. Are they violent when challenged?

Impact: Violence, whether verbal, emotional, or physical, is a direct **violation of covenantal love.** When correction leads to aggression, the home becomes a **hostile, unsafe spiritual environment.** It leads to:

- Deep trauma in children
- Fear of disagreement
- Emotional numbness or rebellion

Violence masquerading under religious language is particularly damaging because it **attaches pain to God's name.**

---

7. Are they involved in Freemasonry or other secret organizations?

Impact: Freemasonry is an **idolatrous covenant system** that opens spiritual doors to deception, perversion, and control. When present in a family:

- It establishes a **false covering**—a counterfeit authority rooted in secrecy and allegiance to other gods.
- Children may struggle with identity, rejection, or spiritual torment.
- The home experiences spiritual heaviness and dysfunction.

This is a **significant portal** for generational bondage, especially in areas of abuse, secrecy, and distorted spiritual authority.

---

8. Will they disparage someone of a different mindset?

Impact: This produces **an atmosphere of spiritual elitism and judgment.** It discourages unity and:

- Prevents honest dialogue

- Shuts down growth or new revelation
- Creates fear around learning or asking questions

It cultivates a home where **only one voice is validated**, leading to emotional control and intellectual/spiritual immaturity in the rest of the family.

Summary: How This Spiritually Destroys the Family

When these traits are present, the family becomes a **counterfeit church structure**, where:

- Legalism replaces love
- Fear replaces trust
- Control replaces spiritual leadership
- Appearance replaces intimacy with God

It creates **spiritual orphans within the home**, even if the family outwardly claims to be "faith based."

Personal Court Case

for the Removal of the Crown of Secrets

Father, I ask to step into Your Court of Mercy, through Jesus, on behalf of me and my generations. I ask that the accuser of the brethren be brought in as well as our generational line, from both sides of the family, and those who are with us by blood, marriage, adoption, civil or religious covenant, from Your hand in the garden and all the way forward as far as it needs to go, as well as my cloud of witnesses.

I want to repent on behalf of myself and my generation, who kept secrets and took this crown willingly. I reveled in harlotry, took on shame, co-labored with deception, allowed it to mock, and caused our own silencing of Your voice. As a governing son, forgive us and our generations for the secrets and for even having secrets about other people and using those secrets against them.

I repent for not taking this crown off our own heads, not confessing our sins one to another so that we could be healed, not confessing these things to you. We harbored them in our hearts and acted like you didn't know. I repent for where we acted as if you couldn't see, and for keeping a secret. And we even smiled about it and reveled in it.

Forgive us and our generations, and forgive us where we took the throne and the seat of Freemasonry within our generations and did not present the throne and the crown to you.

I take it, and I crush it—this inferior crown under our feet—the head of the snake, the head of this dragon, I crush it and present to you the throne and request that the angels utterly destroy it, and the altar, and the idols of secrecy be judged in Your court this day as I repent on behalf of the generations for they did not know what they were doing. I ask that a complete capture of every demonic spirit that was used be made. Forgive us where your voice through us was silenced.

Because of this, I ask that angels crush shame and regret, and I ask for the amendment of "As If It Never Were" as your blood pours through our generations, that the angels would go and remove every single Crown of Secrets in the bloodline and destroy it.

Forgive us when we uncovered the secrets of others and brought them shame because of the knowledge we had. I accept Father, the scripture that everything that is done in secret is brought to light—your light. I ask this in the name of Jesus.

I thank You, Father, I thank You, Jesus, and I thank you, John, for your transparency as we learn that transparency is a Godly Quality—no secrets.

I repent for all cooperation with Baal in any form at any time. I turn our back to the altar of Baal and ask angels to destroy every altar of Baal. I ask for a divorce from Baal, Lucifer, the red dragon, the Book of Magic, and any ungodly attraction. I ask that all debris associated with this cooperation with Baal be removed and destroyed on our behalf. I remove the regalia associated with this ungodly marriage covenant and request to be clothed in robes of righteousness.

I request that the head of this snake be cut off from the other heads and this dragon.

I ask that you please destroy and burn this inferior crown which is set on the seven-headed dragon, the dragon, its seven heads, its inferior crowns, thrones, mantles, scepters, altars, spiritual residue, essences, and debris, in Jesus' name.

I ask that the Superior Crowns of the Kingdom of Heaven be placed upon our heads, overturning the enormity of our sins.

I ask for renewed authorization for every crown restored to us, and those to be restored today in Your court, and the release of every mantle, throne, scepter, altar, anointing, and Glory.

I ask for Your righteous verdict or further counsel.

[If further counsel is advised, follow these instructions. Once you have received a righteous verdict, begin the following segment:]

I speak to the earth that every one of our generations who stepped upon you, even those related to us by blood, marriage, adoption, civil or religious covenant.

Earth, I have received a righteous verdict from the Courts of Heaven this day. I bless you to hear the word of the Lord. I bless you to swallow up the iniquity and the egregious sins of self-deception and wearing these inferior crowns. Swallow up every word and deed that was done upon you. Swallow the innocent bloodshed, sexual sins, moving of the boundary stones, worship of ourselves, idol worship, occultic worship, theft... every sin under the sun that Jesus died for. I charge you to swallow it up and bless you to your original design. I bless you to see the governing sons and to begin blessing us. Begin pouring out your riches of abundance of truth and life.

I request the blood of Jesus to cover every place this was done upon you or in you. I speak to the frequencies of the wind to blow away the evil, to the water to drown it, and to the fire to burn it. I speak to you to return to your original design as the Lord had created you. The Earth is the Lord's, and its fullness belongs to the Lord.

I speak peace. I thank the Just Judge. I thank You, Jesus, the author and the finisher of our faith, for the Crowns of Righteousness and the Crown of Love that trump this inferior crown.

As a governing son, I pick up these Superior Crowns, place them upon our heads, and ask you to help us rule. I commission the angels to render these righteous verdicts in the spirit and the natural. I commission the angels to put this on record.

Thank you, Just Judge, for honoring us and trusting us with the responsibility of wearing these Crowns of Love and Righteousness. Thank you for helping us occupy the *territory you assigned us. I don't take this lightly and ask for supernatural assistance and help daily to govern well as Your sons, in the name of Jesus.*

As a son, I call in the treasure that has been lost from the north, the south, the east, and the west in every age, realm, dimension, and time to fill the capacity of this section.

I ask that all of this be done in time and out of time, and in every age, realm, and dimension, and that all of the spiritual debris, residue, and essences that were left behind by this inferior crown and the spirits that came with it be destroyed utterly. I thank You, Father, for what you did, Jesus, for giving us authority and dominion here.

Court Case
for the Removal of the Crown of Secrets
Off of Someone

Father, I ask to step into Your Court of Mercy, on behalf of_____ through Jesus, on behalf of them and their generations.

I ask that the accuser of the brethren be brought in as well as our generational line, from both sides of the family, and those who are with us by blood, marriage, adoption, civil or religious covenant, from Your hand in the garden and all the way forward as far as it needs to go, as well as my cloud of witnesses.

I want to repent on behalf of them and their generations, who kept secrets and took this crown willingly. They reveled in harlotry, took on shame, co-labored with deception, allowed it to mock, and caused their silencing of Your voice. As a governing son, forgive them and their generations for the secrets and for even having secrets about other people and using those secrets against them.

I repent on their behalf for them not taking this crown off their own heads, not confessing their sins one to another so that they could be healed, not confessing these things to you. They harbored them in their hearts and acted like you didn't know. I repent where they acted like you couldn't see, and where they kept secrets. And they even smiled about it and reveled in it.

Forgive them and their generations, and forgive them where they took the throne and the seat of Freemasonry within their generations and did not present the throne and the crown to you.

As a governing son, I take it and I crush this inferior crown under their feet—I crush the head of this dragon and present to you the throne and request that the angels utterly destroy it, the altar(s), and the idols of secrecy. May they be judged in Your court this day as I repent on behalf of them and their generations, for they did not know what they were doing. I ask for a complete capture of every demonic spirit that was used to be made. Forgive us where your voice through them was silenced.

Because of this, I ask that angels crush shame and regret, and I ask for the amendment of "As If It Never Were" as your blood pours through their generations, that the angels would go and remove every single Crown of Secrets in the bloodline and destroy it.

Forgive them when they uncovered other people and brought them shame because of the secret they knew. Father, I accept the scripture that everything that is done in secret is brought to light—your light. I ask this in the name of Jesus.

I repent for all cooperation with Baal in any form at any time. I turn our back to the altar of Baal and ask angels to destroy every altar of Baal. I ask for a divorce from Baal, Lucifer, the red dragon, the Book of Magic, and any ungodly attraction. I ask that all debris associated with this cooperation with Baal be removed and destroyed on their behalf. I remove the regalia associated with this ungodly marriage covenant and request to be clothed in robes of righteousness.

I request that the head of this snake be cut off from the other heads and this dragon.

I ask that you please destroy and burn this inferior crown which is set on the seven-headed dragon, the dragon, its seven heads, its inferior crowns, thrones, mantles, scepters, altars, spiritual residue, essences, and debris, in Jesus' name.

I ask that the Superior Crowns of the Kingdom of Heaven be placed upon our heads, overturning the enormity of our sins.

I ask for renewed authorization for every crown restored to us, and those to be restored today in Your court, and the release of every mantle, throne, scepter, altar, anointing, and Glory.

I ask for Your righteous verdict or further counsel.

[If further counsel is advised, follow these instructions. Once you have received a righteous verdict, begin the following segment:]

I speak to the earth that every one of their generations who stepped upon you, even those related to them by blood, marriage, adoption, civil or religious covenant.

Earth, I have received a righteous verdict from the Courts of Heaven this day. I bless you to hear the word of the Lord. I bless you to swallow up the iniquity and the egregious sins of self-deception and wearing these inferior crowns. Swallow up every word and deed that was done upon you. Swallow the innocent bloodshed, sexual sins, moving of the boundary stones, worship of ourselves, idol worship, occultic worship, theft... every sin under the sun that Jesus died for. I charge you to swallow it up and bless you to your original design. I *bless you to see the governing sons and to begin blessing them. Begin pouring out your riches of abundance of truth and life.*

I request the blood of Jesus to cover every place this was done upon you or in you. I speak to the frequencies of the wind to blow away the evil, to the water to drown it, and to the fire to burn it. I speak to you to return to your original design as the Lord had created you. The Earth is the Lord's, and its fullness belongs to the Lord.

I speak peace to you. I thank the Just Judge. I thank You, Jesus, the author and the finisher of our faith, for the Crowns of Righteousness and the Crown of Love that trump this inferior crown.

As a governing son, I pick up these Superior Crowns, place them upon their heads, and ask you to help them rule. I commission the angels to render these righteous verdicts in the spirit and the natural. I commission the angels to put this on record.

Thank you, Just Judge, for honoring us and trusting us with the responsibility of wearing these Crowns of Love and Righteousness. Thank you for helping us occupy the territory you assigned us. I don't take this lightly and ask for supernatural assistance and help daily to govern well as Your sons, in the name of Jesus.

As a son, I call in the treasure that has been lost to them and their generations from the north, the south, the east, and the west in every age, realm, dimension, and time to fill the capacity of this section.

I ask that all of this be done in time and out of time, and in every age, realm, and dimension, and that all of the spiritual debris, residue, and essences that were left behind by this inferior crown and the spirits that came with it be destroyed utterly. I thank You, Father, for what you did, Jesus, for giving us authority and dominion here.

However, Mark 4:22 says:

*For there **is nothing that is hidden that won't be disclosed,** and **there is no secret that won't be brought out into the light!** (Emphasis mine)*

Instructions to the Sons:

- Remove and utterly destroy this crown from your heads. It is unbecoming of a son.
- Repent for any involvement with this crown at any time, in any fashion, in any place.
- You are to govern this crown, then remove it, then destroy it.
- Crush this serpent under your feet.

Chapter 11
The False Crown of Antichrist

This crown is full of pomp and circumstance. There is an *elitism* to those who wear this crown. They have a 'Better than you' attitude." It looks down at people.

It has an air of superiority and a superiority complex, not unlike the Sadducees and teachers of the Law in the New Testament. This is the crown that the antichrist will wear.

Those who wear this crown *are indoctrinated.* It has multiple purposes. It works with the Crown of Secrets and the Crown of Deceit, and those who wear it can easily put on the Crown of Deception.

This crown clings to the cross, but in a defiled manner. It is superstitious, seeks fame, is pretentious, full of pride, lofty, arrogant, and judgmental. This crown *has infiltrated the church*. This crown calls in the Delilahs, the Jezebels, and the Ahab's. It has the deadliest bite. In its bite, there are many poisons. This crown *has led more astray* than any of the other crowns. That's what makes it noteworthy. This is the Crown of Antichrist. It embodies false religion. It has a realm.

> *It is the Crown of Antichrist,*
> *there is a Realm of Antichrist*
> *and a Spirit of Antichrist*
> *as well as an Office of Antichrist.*

Many would believe that the unsaved wear this crown, but it is upon those in the church, those with the deadly bite, and upon those who co-conspire with the *spirit*, the *office*, and the *realm* of the antichrist.

It has polluted the church—the ecclesia. Those who are bitten by those who wear this crown often leave the Body of Christ and never return. Over the last several years, you have probably heard or been aware of pastors who have suddenly announced they no longer believe in God. They have taken this crown.

> *Its main goal and focus*
> *are to bring an end*
> *to the embodiment of the church.*

It wants to stop the church dead in its tracks. It will convince people that what Jesus did on the cross and at the resurrection was insufficient. It tells you that Jesus might do it for someone else, but it won't work for you. It denies the power of the resurrection, although it pretends to believe in the power of the resurrection.

> *To deal with it, remove not only its mantle, the crown, and its seat, which is a throne, but also the Delilah's.*

The Delilahs aim to undermine the influence of those working for the Kingdom. It wants them to become eunuchs.

Focus on repentance on behalf of those in the body of Christ who have been elevated to positions and seats of power, and those who have tolerated Jezebel.[8] *Close the portal, remove its garments (false mantles), and request that the head of this snake be cut off from the rest.* It empowers and emboldens those whose lust *is* power and greed, and it enslaves those under it.

> *You must break off the chains of enslavement from this crown for the people.*

---

[8] See Revelation 2:20 – toleration of Jezebel implies toleration of sexual sin in essentially any form, self-gratification, pornography, fornication, adultery, incest, homosexuality, bestiality, etc.

It may appear harmless on the surface, but its bite is deadly and poisonous. It will weave a web of lies and suggest weaknesses in those who lead the Body of Christ, suggesting that God has specially anointed them to fix all the problems in their church. They are cunning and beguiling.

One of the ways it operates in conjunction with the Crown of Secrets is through the infiltration of Freemasonry and the Eastern Star within the church. Many spiritual leaders, pastors, and clergy are Freemasons or are involved in the Eastern Star. This crown will reach over and place the Crown of Deceit or Deception on people's heads.

This crown has an office, too—the Office of the Crown of Antichrist. This crown is specifically designed to work in conjunction with the Crown of Secrets and the Crown of Deceit or Deception. It will cause you to be delusional, have delusions of grandeur, and be secretive. How many pastors and how many churches have been covered in secrets?"

If you have found yourself involved in a church that is secretive, understand that a common secret that churches infiltrated by Freemasonry have is that of child abuse and pedophilia. You want to remove yourself from that environment as quickly as possible. They will attempt to keep you in the circle by offering positions of power within the church, but it is merely a means to ensnare you.

It's not just about removing this crown; you must *remove its mantle, destroy the seat,* and *close the portal,* for it opens portals of deception within the church. It self-justifies the abuse of children as some perverted duty of the adults (particularly the men) to "break them in" sexually. You must *break the chains from those who have been impacted or who have been in agreement with one who wears this crown,* and *those who were over you.*

This may involve ownership claims upon those who have become victims of their wicked works, which you can resolve in the Court of Titles and Deeds. Pay attention to sudden behavioral changes in your children. These often indicate some secretive behavior has affected them. Waste no time in excising yourself from a church environment such as this.

Steps to Freedom from the Crown of Antichrist.

To remove this crown, you must:

1. Remove its mantle.
2. Destroy the seat.
3. Close the portal.
4. Break the chains.

Identifying the False Crown of Antichrist

- Do they carry an unspoken belief that they are spiritually superior to others in your business or team?
- Do they often look down on or discredit believers who don't align with their exact views or methods?
- Do they view themselves as specially anointed to fix or control spiritual environments?
- Do they expect submission from others but resist being accountable to anyone?
- Do they use religious language to justify manipulation, control, or emotional domination?
- Do they appear deeply spiritual in public but operate in secrecy, control, or pride in private?
- Have they ever twisted Scripture to elevate my authority or silence others?
- Have they partnered (directly or indirectly) with secret societies like Freemasonry or the Eastern Star?
- Are they uncomfortable with intercession, the prophetic, or spontaneous worship that they can't control?
- Do they secretly crave fame, attention, or religious recognition?
- Do they wear titles and mantles to elevate myself above others, rather than serve?

How Do These Characteristics Affect Families

This is a piercing and prophetic list—one that cuts to the core of **spiritual hypocrisy and religious control**. When these characteristics manifest in a family setting, especially within a parent, spouse, or spiritual leader, they cause **deep, multi-generational wounds**. These behaviors do more than create dysfunction—they **pollute the spiritual atmosphere**, silence identity, and disfigure the family's view of God.

Let's walk through how each one **negatively impacts a family**:

1. Do they carry an unspoken belief that they are spiritually superior to others in the family?

Impact: This creates a spiritual caste system in the home. Children or spouses are made to feel *less than*, unable to "measure up" to the perceived spiritual standard. This fosters:

- **Shame-based obedience**
- **Stifled spiritual growth**
- A false belief that closeness to God is only for the "elite"

2. Do they often look down on or discredit family members who don't align with their exact views or methods?

Impact: This crushes the **diversity of spiritual expression** and silences differing gifts or insights. It leads to:

- Emotional distancing
- Suppressed creativity and spiritual calling
- A distorted view of unity as *uniformity*

3. Do they view themselves as specially anointed to fix or control spiritual environments?

Impact: This person may feel they are the "Holy Spirit" for the family, constantly correcting, instructing, or dominating. It causes:

- Others to hide their struggles or questions
- A culture of fear or hesitation
- Resistance to genuine transformation because of spiritual pressure

4. Do they expect submission from others but resist being accountable to anyone?

Impact: This double standard breaks trust. Children learn that **authority means domination, not servanthood.** It invites:

- Bitterness
- Rebellion or fear-based compliance
- The breakdown of mutual respect

5. Do they use religious language to justify manipulation, control, or emotional domination?

Impact: This is **spiritual abuse.** It weaponizes Scripture and God's name to get compliance. It results in:

- Deep confusion about God's character
- Long-term trauma in children or spouses
- Guilt-based submission and the loss of personal will

6. Do they appear deeply spiritual in public but operate in secrecy, control, or pride in private?

Impact: This hypocrisy teaches children that faith is **a mask, not a lifestyle.** It causes:

- Emotional dissonance ("Which version of Mom/Dad is real?")
- Rejection of faith altogether
- Trust issues in relationships and church communities

7. Have they ever twisted Scripture to elevate their authority or silence others?

Impact: This corrupts the purpose of the Word and forms **unholy soul ties** in the home. It teaches:

- That questioning leadership = rebellion
- That truth can be selectively applied
- That God agrees with control and manipulation

---

8. Have they partnered (directly or indirectly) with secret societies like Freemasonry or the Eastern Star?

Impact: These covenants invite **spiritual contamination** into the home. They open doors to:

- Confusion, fear, and spiritual resistance in children
- An atmosphere of secrecy and spiritual heaviness
- Generational strongholds in identity, sexuality, and authority

---

9. Are they uncomfortable with intercession, the prophetic, or spontaneous worship that they can't control?

Impact: This suppresses **Holy Spirit-led expression** in the home. Children may learn:

- That God only moves through control
- That the supernatural is suspicious
- That worship must follow a script, not flow from the heart

---

10. Do they secretly crave fame, attention, or religious recognition?

Impact: The home becomes about *them*, not the Lord. This produces:

- A performance culture
- Constant striving for approval
- Competition and comparison within the family

---

11. Do they wear titles and mantles to elevate themselves above others, rather than serve?

Impact: Servanthood is replaced with **religious hierarchy.** Children learn:

- That authority is about elevation, not humility
- That titles matter more than fruit
- That love is earned, not given

The Bigger Picture: What It Produces in the Family

These traits collectively establish a **False Throne in the Home**—a spiritual seat of control, fear, and performance where:

- Love is conditional
- Questions are punished
- The Holy Spirit is grieved
- Identity is stifled
- And generational cycles of spiritual abuse are perpetuated

Children raised in this environment often:

- Reject the church or faith
- Become a perfectionist or a rebel
- Struggle with fear, shame, or performance-based identity
- Need extensive **inner healing and deconstruction of false theology**

Personal Court Case

for the Removal of the Crown of Antichrist

Father, I ask to step into the Mercy Court of Heaven to receive Mercy in our time of need. I request the accuser of the brethren be brought in as well as my entire generations and everyone related to me by blood, marriage, adoption, civil or religious covenant, from

Your hand in the garden, and all the way forward as far as it needs to go, as well as my cloud of witnesses.

Your Honor, I agree with the adversary that my generations bowed our knees to this dragon, accepted the inferior crowns, and wore them proudly. I repent for the spirit of antichrist we bore and the inferior crown we took upon our heads. I repent for the pomp and circumstance, elitism, better than you attitude, superiority complex, indoctrination we took on, as well as the indoctrination of others; I repent for embodying a false religion and for 'biting' those we were in stewardship over, releasing the poison. I repent for working with the false Crown of Delusion as well as the false Crown of Secrets. I repent for all of the secrets this inferior crown bore that we agreed with.

I repent for conspiring with the office, realm, and spirit of antichrist, for embodying it. I repent for participating in exploiting, polluting, and poisoning the church, the body, and the ecclesia. I repent for being a part of ending the lives of bodies of ecclesias, people, and churches. I repent for allowing, tolerating, being in league with, and cooperating with the Delilah spirit, Jezebel, and Ahab. I repent for opening up an evil portal and for creating evil timelines for us, our generations, and for others. I repent for taking on this mantle, sitting in the seat of office, and ruling unjustly over your people. I repent for seeking to be elevated to positions and seats of power, or where we, who wore this inferior crown, elevated those who should never have been elevated. I repent for the pride and for lusting after power and greed.

I repent for the false clinging to the cross, the defilement and mockery of it, for seeking fame, being pretentious, full of pride, lofty, arrogant, and judging others. I repent for embodying false religion, for promoting and esteeming it. Forgive us and our generations for infiltrating the church, bringing this inferior crown and elevating others to it. Forgive us for leading others astray.

I request your blood, Jesus, the amendment of "As If It Never Were," the destruction of the seat/office/throne, the closing of the portal, and the removal of the garments. Please remove its mantle, destroy the seat, and close the portal. I ask that you break the chains from those who have been impacted or who have agreed with those who have worn this inferior crown over the generations, and those whom we were over. Please have these destroyed.

I request that the chains attached to us and our generations be cut, severed, destroyed, dismantled, and the ashes of them be brought to Jesus. I request a complete destruction, annulment, cancellation, and overturning of the office of the Crown of Antichrist, in the name of Jesus.

I also request that the angels clean up the spiritual debris, essences, and residues in time, out of time and in every age, realm, and dimension to infinity. Burn it and give the ashes to Jesus.

I ask that you please destroy and burn this inferior crown which is set on the seven-headed dragon, the dragon, its seven heads, its inferior crowns, thrones, mantles, scepters, altars, spiritual residue, essences, and debris, in Jesus' name.

I ask that the Superior Crowns of the Kingdom of Heaven be placed upon our heads, overturning the enormity of our sins.

I ask for renewed authorization for every crown restored to us, and those to be restored today in Your court, and the release of every mantle, throne, scepter, altar, anointing, and Glory.

I ask for Your righteous verdict or further counsel.

[If further repentance is needed, follow the instructions of the court.]

With our righteous verdict in hand, I speak to the Earth. I speak to you that every one of our generations who stepped upon you, even those related to us by blood, marriage, adoption, civil or religious covenant. Earth, I have received a righteous verdict from the Courts of Heaven this day.

I bless you to hear the word of the Lord. I bless you to swallow up the iniquity and the egregious sins of wearing these inferior crowns. Swallow up every word and deed that was done upon you. Swallow the innocent bloodshed, sexual sins, moving of the boundary stones, worship of ourselves, idol worship, occultic worship, theft... every sin under the sun that Jesus died for.

I charge you to swallow it up, and I bless you to your original design; I bless you to see the governing sons and to begin blessing us. Begin pouring out your riches of the abundance of the truth of life. I request the blood of Jesus to cover every place this was done upon you, in you. I speak to the frequencies of the wind to blow away the evil. To the water, to drown it, and to the fire to burn it. I speak to you to return to your original design, as the Lord created you and the earth. The earth is the Lord's, and the fullness of it belongs to the Lord.

I speak peace and I thank You, Jesus. I thank the Just Judge. I thank You, Jesus, the author and the finisher of our faith. I commission the angels to render these righteous verdicts in the spirit and the natural.

I commission the angels to put this on record. Thank you, Just Judge, for honoring us and trusting us with the responsibility of wearing the Crown of Love and the Crown of Righteousness. Thank you for helping us occupy the territory you assigned us. I don't take this lightly and ask for supernatural assistance and help daily to govern well as Your sons, in the name of Jesus.

As a son, I call in the treasure that has been lost from the north, the south, the east, and the west in every age, realm, dimension, and time to fill the capacity of this section.

I am grateful to Heaven for revealing the red dragon, its inferior crowns, and its mission. I am grateful that Revelation tells us that this dragon has been pierced by God himself. Thank you for being so kind in helping us overcome the word of our testimony and the blood of the lamb.

I ask that all of this be done in time and out of time, and in every age, realm, and dimension, and that all of the spiritual debris, residue, and essences that were left behind by this inferior crown and the spirits that came with it be destroyed utterly. I thank You, Father, for what you did, Jesus, for giving us authority and dominion here.

Court Case
for the Removal of the Crown of Antichrist
Off of Someone

Father, I ask to step into the Mercy Court of Heaven on behalf of _____ to receive Mercy in our time of need. I request the accuser of the brethren be brought in as well as them and their entire generations and everyone related to them by blood, marriage, adoption, civil or religious covenant, from Your hand in the garden, and all the way forward as far as it needs to go, as well as my cloud of witnesses.

Your Honor, I agree with the adversary that they and their generations bowed their knees to this dragon, accepted the inferior crowns, and wore them proudly. I repent for the spirit of antichrist they bore and the inferior crown they took upon their heads. I repent for the pomp and circumstance, elitism, indoctrination, better-than-you attitude, and superiority complex we took on, as well as the indoctrination of others; I repent for embodying a false religion and for 'biting' those they were in stewardship over, releasing the poison. I repent for working with the false Crown of Delusion as well as the false Crown of Secrets. I repent for all of the secrets this inferior crown bore that they agreed with.

I repent for conspiring with the office, realm, and spirit of antichrist, for embodying it. I repent for participating in exploiting, polluting, and poisoning the church, the body, and the ecclesia. I repent for being a part of ending the lives of bodies of ecclesias, people, and churches. I repent for allowing, tolerating, being in league with, and cooperating with the Delilah spirit, Jezebel, and Ahab. We repent for opening up an evil portal and for creating evil timelines for us, our generations, and for others. We repent for taking on this mantle, sitting on the seat, the throne, and in the office of antichrist and ruling unjustly over your people. I repent for seeking to be elevated to positions and seats of power, or where they, who wore this inferior crown, elevated those who should not ever have been elevated. I repent for the pride and for lusting after power and greed.

I repent for the false clinging to the cross, the defilement and mockery of it, for seeking fame, being pretentious, full of pride, lofty, arrogant, and judging others. I repent for embodying false religion, for promoting and esteeming it. Forgive us and our generations for infiltrating the church, bringing this inferior crown and elevating others to it. Forgive us for leading others astray.

I request your blood, Jesus, the amendment of "As If It Never Were," the destruction of the seat/office/throne, the closing of the portal, and the removal of the garments. Please remove its mantle, destroy the seat, and close the portal. I ask that you break the chains from those who have been impacted or who have agreed with those who have worn this inferior crown over the generations, and those whom they were over. Please have these destroyed.

I request that the chains attached to us and our generations be cut, severed, destroyed, dismantled, and the ashes of them be brought to Jesus. I request a complete destruction, annulment, cancellation, and overturning of the office of the Crown of Antichrist, in the name of Jesus.

I also request that the angels clean up the spiritual debris, essences, and residues in time, out of time, and in every age, realm, and dimension to infinity. Burn it and give the ashes to Jesus.

I ask for Your righteous verdict or further counsel.

[If further repentance is needed, follow the instructions of the court.]

With our righteous verdict in hand, I speak to the Earth. I speak to you that every one of our generations who stepped upon you, even those related to us by blood, marriage, adoption, civil or religious covenant. Earth, I have received a righteous verdict from the Courts of Heaven this day.

I bless you to hear the word of the Lord. I bless you to swallow up the iniquity and the egregious sins of wearing these inferior crowns. Swallow up every word and deed that was done upon you. Swallow the innocent bloodshed, sexual sins, moving of the boundary stones, worship of ourselves, idol worship, occultic worship, theft... every sin under the sun that Jesus died for.

I charge you to swallow it up, and I bless you to your original design; I bless you to see the governing sons and to begin blessing us. Begin pouring out your riches of the abundance of the truth of life. I request the blood of Jesus to cover every place this was done upon you, in you. I speak to the frequencies of the wind to blow away the evil. To the water, to drown it, and to the fire to burn it. I speak to you to return to your original design, as the Lord created you and the earth. The earth is the Lord's, and the fullness of it belongs to the Lord.

I speak peace and I thank You, Jesus. I thank the Just Judge. I thank You, Jesus, the author and the finisher of our faith. I commission the angels to render these righteous verdicts in the spirit and the natural.

I commission the angels to put this on record. Thank you, Just Judge, for honoring us and trusting us with the responsibility of wearing the Crown of Love and the Crown of Righteousness. Thank you for helping us occupy the territory you assigned us. I don't take this lightly and ask for supernatural assistance and help daily to govern well as Your sons, in the name of Jesus.

As a son, I call in the treasure that has been lost from the north, the south, the east, and the west in every age, realm, dimension, and time to fill the capacity of this section.

I am grateful to Heaven for revealing the red dragon, its inferior crowns, and its mission. I am grateful that Revelation tells us that God himself has pierced this dragon. Thank you for your kindness in helping us overcome the word of our testimony and the blood of the lamb.

I ask that all of this be done in time and out of time, and in every age, realm, and dimension, and that all of the spiritual debris, residue, and essences that were left behind by this inferior crown and the spirits that came with it be destroyed utterly. I thank You, Father, for what you did, Jesus, for giving us authority and dominion here.

Solutions

- Remove not only its mantle, the crown, and its seat, which is a throne, but also the Delilah's.
- Focus on the repentance work of those in the body of Christ who have been elevated to positions and seats of power. To those who have ruling and rank over the people, and to those who have tolerated Jezebel.
- Close the portal.
- Remove its garments.
- Request that the head of this snake be cut off from the rest.
- You must break off the chains of enslavement from this crown for the people.

Chapter 12

The False Crown of Devouring

The seventh false crown is the *Crown of Devouring*. This head of the dragon is seeking whomever he may devour. He sniffs out the weak and those on the edge. He seeks whom he can devour. The dragon hunts after the sons to place this crown upon them. This is a fierce crown in league with the sons of perdition—the ones that have given themselves over to darkness, also referred to as Sons of Belial or S.O.B.'s.

Because sin leaves a stench, the dragon hunts you. He follows the trail of the stench of sin. If sin is in your life, he can smell you.

Jude 1:17-23:

> *17 But you, beloved, remember the words which were spoken before by the apostles of our Lord Jesus Christ: 18 how they told you that there would be **mockers** in the last time who would **walk according to their own ungodly lusts.***

*¹⁹ These are **sensual persons**, who **cause divisions, not having the Spirit**.*

*²⁰ But you, beloved, building yourselves up on your most holy faith, praying in the Holy Spirit, ²¹ keep yourselves in the love of God, looking for the mercy of our Lord Jesus Christ unto eternal life. ²² And on some have compassion, making a distinction; ²³ but others save with fear, pulling them out of the fire, **hating even the garment defiled by the flesh**. (Emphasis mine)*

Notice that Jude details some of their deeds:

- They mock
- They walk according to their own ungodly lusts
- They are sensual people
- They cause divisions
- They walk in the wrong spirit

Some follow *darkness,* while others fall into it. There is a difference. This dragon hunts both. Most don't return when this crown is put upon their head. It's lethal. That's what devouring does.

With this crown, you lose all sensibility and sense of oneness.

The most hardened of hearts wear this crown.

This isn't just an atheistic view; this is *a hatred of God*, a turning away, and the true son of perdition. It's not like the average sinner wears this crown. This dragon *seeks to devour common sense* and commonalities in people's lives so *they cannot hear the voice of God or see God.* That is what this dragon seeks—to devour the truth. The darkest of the dark wear this crown.

To watch the news, you probably have said, "They have lost their minds!" That is what this devouring crown does. You lose all sense of reason. If you encounter someone *with whom you cannot reason and who appears to lack common sense*, this individual is likely to be under the influence of this crown.

It's not the average atheist or sinner who wears this crown. This is like the deepest, darkest, blackest-hearted people. The ones that consume babies and murder and are on a path of what we would call the evil ones. An example would be Adolf Hitler or some of his assistants. It is sniffing out sin. It works in tandem with all other crowns because *it seeks to devour*.

2 Thessalonians 2:3:

> *Let no one deceive you by any means; for that day will not come unless the falling away comes first, and the man of sin is revealed, the* **son of perdition***. (Emphasis mine)*

John 17:12:

While I was with them in the world, I kept them in Your name. Those whom You gave Me I have kept; and none of them is lost except **the son of perdition,** *that the Scripture might be fulfilled. (Emphasis mine)*

There is no light in them.
There is only darkness.

Perdition typically refers to a state of perishing, being lost, dying, or destruction.

They have no light in them. The dragon seeks someone he can devour and take to hell with him.

When you sin,
it begins sniffing you out.

He roams about and seeks to devour things. He has been looking for the crowns he can claim. The other false crowns must be removed before addressing this one.

Atheists and those family members who don't believe they are wearing this crown, but they have purposefully stepped over into something really dark—*they have no conscience.*

Identifying the False Crown of Devouring

- Are they hiding secret sins?
- Are they heavily involved in darkness?
- Do their words express wickedness?
- Are they conniving?
- Do they have a hardened heart?
- Do they mock?
- Do they have sensibility?
- Do they have a sense of oneness?
- Do they have a hard heart?
- Do they seek to devour common sense?
- Do they seek to devour commonalities in people's lives?
- Do they cause divisions?
- Do they despise the truth?
- Do they have no conscience?
- Are they filled with darkness?
- Have they stepped into a depth of darkness purposefully?

How Do These Characteristics Affect Families

This list represents a deeply entrenched and spiritually dangerous condition—what we might call **a throne of willful darkness and deception operating within a household.** When a parent, spouse, or family leader carries these traits, the impact on the family isn't just dysfunction—it becomes **destruction of identity, truth, connection, and spiritual covering.** Let's walk through each one to reveal how it fractures the family structure and poisons the generational line.

---

1. Are they hiding secret sins?

Impact: Secret sin erodes spiritual authority. It opens doors to demonic access and **invites confusion, mistrust, and oppression** into the home. Family members may feel unsettled without knowing why. This silence creates spiritual fog and unspoken distance.

---

2. Are they heavily involved in darkness?

Impact: This doesn't just damage relationships—it corrupts the spiritual atmosphere. Involvement with witchcraft, occult practices, perversion, or hatred **pollutes the spiritual covering of the home.** Children may suffer nightmares, oppression, or anxiety without understanding the cause.

---

3. Do their words express wickedness?

Impact: Words carry life or death (Proverbs 18:21). Wicked speech wounds deeply. Sarcasm, curses, accusations, and manipulation **dismantle emotional safety** and instill fear or shame, especially in children.

4. Are they conniving?

Impact: Manipulation, schemes, and secret agendas destroy trust. Family members walk on eggshells, always unsure of the true motive. This cultivates **an environment of control, secrecy, and betrayal.**

5. Do they have a hardened heart?

Impact: A hard heart cannot love deeply or repent. It blocks compassion and leads to **emotional coldness.** Children raised under a hardened parent often suppress emotion or seek love in unsafe places.

6. Do they mock?

Impact: Mockery is verbal abuse dressed in wit. It minimizes others' pain, dreams, or faith. This kills childlike joy and trust in the home, causing **deep shame and spiritual confusion.**

7. Do they have sensibility? (If not)

Impact: A lack of spiritual and emotional awareness can lead to harmful choices. It creates **chaotic or unsafe situations** and prevents wise counsel from taking root. It teaches children to suppress their intuition and discernment.

8. Do they have a sense of oneness? (If not)

Impact: Without unity, the family operates in isolation, focusing on self-preservation. Relationships become **transactional, not relational.** It removes the sense of belonging, warmth, and shared purpose.

9. Do they have a hard heart?

Impact: Repeated for emphasis—it means love cannot grow. A hard-hearted person **shuts down connections**, prioritizes control, and may even take pleasure in causing pain because they are numb to others' emotions.

10. Do they seek to devour common sense?

Impact: This is the spirit of delusion or false wisdom. They twist logic, deny obvious truths, and cause family members to **doubt their sanity.** This creates spiritual gaslighting and mental oppression.

11. Do they seek to devour commonalities in people's lives?

Impact: This breaks unity by sowing division. It isolates individuals from one another. What should bring connection (faith, family, love) becomes a **source of attack, criticism, or ridicule.**

12. Do they cause divisions?

Impact: Division is a demonic strategy to sever covenant bonds. It can turn family members against each other, creating long-term estrangement, emotional distance, and even **generational curses.**

13. Do they despise the truth?

Impact: Truth is the foundation of healthy families. When it's despised, **lies become the default language.** It prevents healing, silences discernment, and makes healthy confrontation impossible.

14. Do they have no conscience?

Impact: Without a conscience, nothing is off-limits. Abuse, manipulation, and betrayal become normalized. This creates **soul-level trauma** and requires deep inner healing and deliverance for restoration.

15. Are they filled with darkness?

Impact: Spiritual darkness blocks revelation, joy, and clarity. It creates a **dense atmosphere of**

confusion, fear, and spiritual dullness. Dreams die. Vision fades. Children grow up either numb or anxious.

16. Have they stepped into a depth of darkness purposefully?

Impact: This is a full-on **alignment with evil.** When someone chooses darkness over light intentionally, they invite principalities into their home. This creates **territorial bondage** that may lead to:

- generational curses
- severe emotional/physical abuse
- spiritual imprisonment
- the silencing of all righteous voices in the home

Summary: What This Produces in the Family

- Fear-based parenting or partnership
- **Emotional or spiritual orphanhood** among children
- **Cycles of control, secrecy, and spiritual abuse**
- **Disconnection from truth and God's presence**
- A house governed by **power, manipulation, and performance**, not love and grace

Children raised under this often:

- Reject church and God completely
- Battle anxiety, fear, or rebellion

- Feel unsafe in all authority relationships
- Need **deliverance, inner healing, and re-parenting** by the Lord

---

Personal Court Case for the Removal of the Crown of Devouring

[Repentance for this crown needs to follow repentance for all the other false crowns.]

Father, I ask to step into Your Court of Mercy to receive mercy in our time of need. I ask that the accuser of the brethren be brought into this court as well as my generations, those related to me by blood, marriage, civil and religious covenant, all the way back to Your hand in the garden and all the way forward as far as it needs to go, and my cloud of witnesses..

Your Honor, this Crown of Devouring cannot be removed until the other crowns are removed. However, I would like to begin the court case process today.

Your Honor, I repent for myself and my generations for partnering, agreeing with, and participating with the darkest of the darkest of sins. I repent that I put myself and our generations in danger of being hunted because of these sins. I repent for our weaknesses in not seeking after God. I repent for our generation's sins that created a stench that the enemy could sniff out.

I repent for living on the edge, allowing this dragon to hunt us and those in our generations. I repent for being in league with the sons of perdition—the ones that have given themselves over to darkness. I repent for losing all sensibility and sense of oneness of our spirit, soul, and body in cooperation with the Lord. I repent for becoming and having the most hardened of hearts. I repent for having deliberately stepped into something dark and for agreeing to have no conscience.

I repent for allowing ourselves to be void of truth. I repent for taking up the other crowns and then wearing this one, the last. I repent for the lust of blood, the drinking of blood, and the eating of flesh from the kingdom of darkness. We are only to take in the blood and body of Christ. I repent for myself and our generations. I repent for the idea of getting near the unholy fire and letting it burn us and for basking in it, allowing it to consume us.

I request that all crowns be destroyed and that this specific crown be fully removed and destroyed, as I have done the repentance work. I request the full removal of this vile crown from our heads as well as from the heads of our generations. I ask that it be burned in the Holy Fire of the Lord God Almighty.

I request the amendment of "As If It Never Were" and ask for restoration in the mighty name of Jesus.

Please burn the spiritual residue, essences, and debris. In Jesus' name, I ask for the Superior Crowns of the Kingdom of Heaven to be placed on our heads, overturning the egregiousness of our sins.

I ask for Your righteous verdict, Your Honor, or further counsel.

[If further counsel is advised, follow these instructions. Once you have received a righteous verdict, begin the following segment:]

I speak to the earth that every one of our generations who stepped upon you, even those related to us by blood, marriage, adoption, civil or religious covenant.

Earth, I have received a righteous verdict from the Courts of Heaven this day. I bless you to hear the word of the Lord. I bless you to swallow up the iniquity and the egregious sins of self-deception and wearing these crowns. Swallow up every word and deed that was done upon you. Swallow the innocent bloodshed, sexual sins, moving of the boundary stones, worship of ourselves, idol worship, occultic worship, theft... every sin under the sun that Jesus died for. I charge you to swallow it up and bless you to your original design. I bless you to see the governing sons and to begin blessing us. Begin pouring out your riches of abundance of truth and life.

I request the blood of Jesus to cover every place this was done upon you or in you. I speak to the frequencies of the wind to blow away the evil, to the water to drown it, and to the fire to burn it. I speak to you to return to your original design as the Lord had created you. The Earth is the Lord's, and its fullness belongs to the Lord.

I speak peace. I thank the Just Judge. I thank You, Jesus, the author and the finisher of our faith, for the Crowns of Righteousness and the Crown of Love that trump this inferior crown.

As a governing son, I pick up these Superior Crowns, place them upon our heads, and ask you to help us rule. I commission the angels to render these righteous verdicts in the spirit and the natural. I commission the angels to put this on record.

Thank you, Just Judge, for honoring us and trusting us with the responsibility of wearing these Crowns of Love and Righteousness. Thank you for helping us occupy the territory you assigned us. I don't take this lightly and ask for supernatural assistance and help daily to govern well as Your sons, in the name of Jesus.

As a son, I call in the treasure that has been lost from the north, the south, the east, and the west in every age, realm, dimension, and time to fill the capacity of this section.

I ask that all of this be done in time and out of time, and in every age, realm, and dimension, and that all of the spiritual debris, residue, and essences that were left behind by this inferior crown and the spirits that came with it be destroyed utterly. I thank You, Father, for what you did, Jesus, for giving us authority and dominion here.

Court Case for the Removal of the Crown of Devouring Off of Someone

[Repentance for this crown needs to follow repentance for all the other false crowns.]

Father, I ask to step into Your Court of Mercy on behalf of _____ to receive mercy in time of need. I ask that the accuser of the brethren be brought into this court as well as their generations, those related to them by blood, marriage, civil and religious covenant, all the way back to Your hand in the garden and all the way forward as far as it needs to go, and their cloud of witnesses.

Your Honor, this Crown of Devouring cannot be removed until the other false crowns are removed. However, I would like to begin the court case process today.

Your Honor, I repent for them and their generations for partnering, agreeing with, and participating with the darkest of the darkest of sins. I repent that they put themselves and their generations in danger of being hunted because of these sins. I repent for their weaknesses in not seeking after God. I repent for the sins of their generations that created a stench the enemy could sniff out.

I repent for them living on the edge, allowing this dragon to hunt them and those in their generations. I repent for them being in league with the sons of perdition—the ones that have given themselves over to darkness. I repent for them losing all sensibility and sense of oneness of our spirit, soul, and body in cooperation with the Lord. I repent for them becoming and having the most hardened of hearts. I repent for them having deliberately stepped into something dark and for agreeing to have no conscience.

I repent for allowing ourselves to be void of truth. I repent for them taking up the other crowns and then wearing this one. I repent for their lust of blood, for their drinking of blood, and the eating of flesh from the kingdom of darkness. We are only to take in the blood and body of Christ. I repent for them and their generations. I repent for the idea of getting near the unholy fire and letting it burn them and for basking in it, allowing it to consume them.

I request that all crowns be destroyed and that this specific crown be entirely removed and destroyed, as I have done the repentance work. I request the complete removal of this vile crown from our heads as well as from the heads of their generations. I ask that it be burned in the Holy Fire of the Lord God Almighty.

I request the amendment of "As If It Never Were" and ask for restoration in the mighty name of Jesus.

Please burn the spiritual residue, essences, and debris. In Jesus' name, I ask for the Superior Crowns of the Kingdom of Heaven to be placed on their heads, overturning the egregiousness of their sins.

I ask for Your righteous verdict, Your Honor, or further counsel.

[If further counsel is advised, follow these instructions. Once you have received a righteous verdict, begin the following segment:]

I speak to the earth that every one of their generations who stepped upon you, even those related to them by blood, marriage, adoption, civil or religious covenant.

Earth, I have received a righteous verdict from the Courts of Heaven this day. I bless you to hear the word of the Lord. I bless you to swallow up the iniquity and the egregious sins of self-deception and wearing these crowns. Swallow up every word and deed that was done upon you. Swallow the innocent bloodshed, sexual sins, moving of the boundary stones, worship of ourselves, idol worship, occultic worship, theft… every sin under the sun that Jesus died for. I charge you to swallow it up and bless you to your original design. I bless you to see the governing sons and to begin blessing us. Begin pouring out your riches of abundance of truth and life.

I request the blood of Jesus to cover every place this was done upon you or in you. I speak to the frequencies of the wind to blow away the evil, to the water to drown it, and to the fire to burn it. I speak to you to return to your original design as the Lord had created you. The Earth is the Lord's, and its fullness belongs to the Lord.

I speak peace. I thank the Just Judge. I thank You, Jesus, the author and the finisher of our faith, for the Crowns of Righteousness and the Crown of Love that trump this inferior crown.

As a governing son, I pick up these Superior Crowns, place them upon their heads, and ask you to help them rule. I commission the angels to render these righteous verdicts in the spirit and the natural. I commission the angels to put this on record.

Thank you, Just Judge, for honoring us and trusting us with the responsibility of wearing these Crowns of Love and Righteousness. Thank you for helping us occupy the territory you assigned us. I don't take this lightly and ask for supernatural assistance and help daily to govern well as Your sons, in the name of Jesus.

As a son, I call in the treasure that has been lost to them and their generations from the north, the south, the east, and the west in every age, realm, dimension, and time to fill the capacity of this section.

I ask that all of this be done in time and out of time, in every age, realm, and dimension, and that all the spiritual debris, residue, and essences left behind by this inferior crown and the spirits that accompanied it be utterly destroyed. I thank You, Father, for what you did, Jesus, for giving us authority and dominion here.

Interaction of the Seven False Crowns

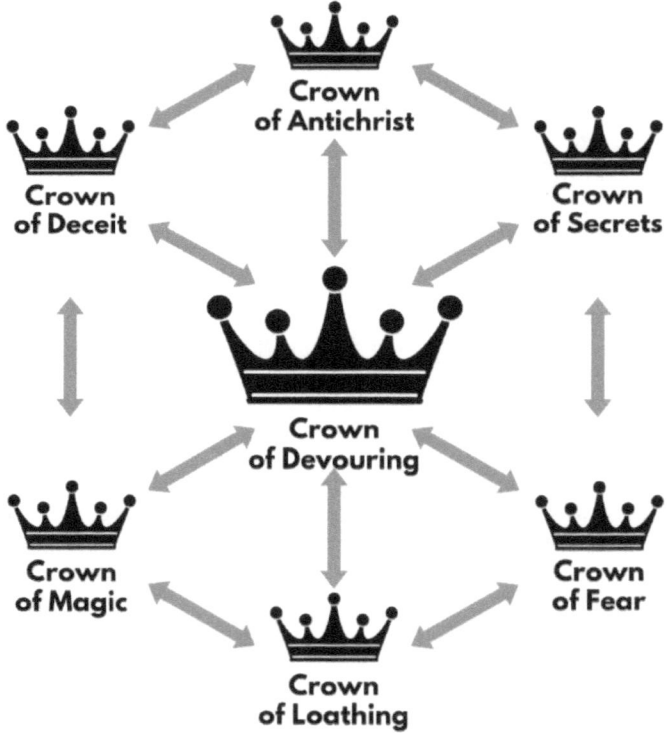

Copyright © 2025 LIfeSpring Publishing

Chapter 13
Gaining Freedom
From False Crowns

If you have worked through the court case for freedom from all seven of the false crowns, you may want to wrap up the court work in this manner:

Personal Court Work

for Freedom from

the Seven False Crowns

Father, I ask to step into Your Court of Crowns. I ask that the accuser of the brethren be brought into this court as well as my generations, those related to me by blood, marriage, civil and religious covenant, all the way back to Your hand in the garden and all the way forward as far as it needs to go.

I ask that the seven-headed dragon be brought in and muzzled and caged. I request that the accuser of the brethren and every Principality, power, demon, ruler of darkness, and evil entity that was associated with the seven-headed dragon, their inferior crowns, mantles, altars, thrones, and scepters, be brought in and gagged as well.

Your Honor, having done repentance work for each of the seven crowns, I ask that the repentance work already accomplished be entered into evidence, and the verdicts be brought into evidence in this court this day. I also request our cloud of witnesses, the angels, and every witness to these events be brought into this court on our behalf.

I request that these seven heads be judged today, for they have inflicted pain, torment, anguish, and untold misery upon Your sons and daughters and the peoples of the earth. They have hindered the growth, abilities, expansion, and work of Your church on Earth. They have murdered, stolen, and destroyed without regard for You, Your sons, or Your purposes in the earth. They have laid evil and egregious crowns on the heads of Your sons to mock not only them but You.

I ask that each head be judged, cut off, and destroyed from our lives, and the damage be undone via the amendment of "As if it Never Were."

I ask that you please burn the inferior Crown of the Beast, which is set above the seven-headed dragon, the dragon, its seven heads, its inferior crowns, thrones, mantles, scepters, altars, spiritual residue, essences, and debris. In Jesus' name, I ask for the Superior Crowns of the Kingdom of Heaven to be placed on our heads, overturning the egregiousness of our sins.

I ask for renewed authorization for every crown restored to us and those to be restored today in Your court.

I am grateful to Heaven for revealing the red dragon, its inferior crowns, associated evil entities, and its mission. I am grateful that Revelation tells us that this dragon has been pierced by God Himself. Thank You for your kindness in helping us overcome the word of our testimony and the blood of the lamb.

I ask that all of this be done in time and out of time, and in every age, realm, and dimension, and that all the spiritual debris, residue, and essences that were left behind by this inferior crown and the spirits that came with it be destroyed utterly. I also ask that these evil entities be judged in Your court this day, in Jesus' name.

I thank You, Father, for what you did, Jesus, for giving us the authority and dominion here.

Court Work
for Freedom from
the Seven False Crowns
for Some Else

Father, I ask to step into Your Court of Crowns on behalf of _____. I ask that the accuser of the brethren be brought into this court as well as them and their generations, those related to us by blood, marriage, civil and religious covenant, all the way back to Your hand in the garden and all the way forward as far as it needs to go.

I ask that the seven-headed dragon be brought in and muzzled and caged. I request that the accuser of the brethren and every Principality, power, demon, ruler of darkness, and evil entity that was associated with the seven-headed dragon, their inferior crowns, mantles, altars, thrones, and scepters, be brought in and gagged as well.

Having done repentance work for each of the seven crowns, Your Honor, I ask that the repentance work already accomplished and the verdicts be brought into evidence in this court this day. I also request that they and their cloud of witnesses, the angels, and every witness to these events be brought into this court on their behalf.

I request that these seven heads be judged today, for they have inflicted pain, torment, anguish, and untold misery upon Your sons and daughters and the peoples of the earth. They have hindered the growth, abilities, expansion, and work of Your church on Earth. They have murdered, stolen, and destroyed without regard for You, Your sons, or Your purposes in the earth. They have laid evil and egregious crowns on the heads of Your sons to mock not only them but You.

I ask that each head be judged, cut off, and destroyed from our lives, and the damage be undone via the amendment of "As if it Never Were."

I ask that You please burn the inferior Crown of the Beast which is set above the seven-headed dragon, the dragon, its seven heads, its inferior crowns, thrones, mantles, scepters, altars, spiritual residue, essences, and debris. In Jesus' name, I ask for the Superior Crowns of the Kingdom of Heaven to be placed on our heads, overturning the egregiousness of our sins.

I ask for renewed authorization for every crown restored to us and those to be restored today in Your court.

I am grateful to Heaven for revealing the red dragon, its inferior crowns, associated evil entities, and its mission. I am grateful that Revelation tells us that God Himself has pierced this dragon. Thank You for Your kindness in helping us overcome the word of our testimony and the blood of the lamb.

I ask that all of this be done in time and out of time, in every age, realm, and dimension, and that all the spiritual debris, residue, and essences left behind by this inferior crown and the spirits that accompanied it be utterly destroyed. I also ask that these evil entities be judged in Your court this day, in the name of Jesus.

I thank You, Father, for what You did, Jesus, for giving us the authority and dominion here.

These seven false crowns are by no means the only ungodly crowns; they are simply seven primary categories of false crowns. These are the biggies. In your intercession, you will uncover and remove other ungodly crowns from these leaders. No matter what the crown's title, the great news is that the Superior Crowns of Heaven always trump it.

———— ∞ ————

Chapter 14
Superior Crowns

Any crown from Heaven is superior to the inferior crowns that Satan has devised or corrupted. We want the inferior false crowns replaced with the Superior Crowns of Heaven.

Where you find an inferior Crown of Strife, you want it removed and replaced with a Superior Crown of the Shalom of God. Where you find an inferior crown of division, you want it removed, the works of the crown destroyed, and place a Crown of the Unity of Heaven in its stead.

Crowns are critical for the sons to understand and for parents to understand and maximize in their own lives and the lives of their children. Authority in one's life can be reborn or reignited by the embrace of crowns. Some crowns come with a cost, while others are a result of the cost. The number of crowns available to the sons is immeasurable, for the Father wants our authority to be immeasurable.

---

*The Father wants to see
every inferior crown
bowing to a Superior Crown.*

The sick man in Acts at the temple gate was wearing a Crown of Sickness, and it needed to be exchanged for a Crown of Wholeness.

When people carry a Crown of Depression or defeat, that inferior crown must bow to the Superior Crown of Hope and Victory. When you see how many are bent low under the weight of an inferior crown, see that inferior crown bowing to a Superior Crown. That is how the will of Heaven manifests. Replace the inferior crowns with Superior Crowns.

Remember, the Word says that in the name of Jesus, every knee will bow, and every tongue will confess the Lordship of Jesus.[9] That is an inferior crown bowing to the Superior Crown.

The Authority of Inferior Crowns

A principle of the Word is that all crowns carry a degree of authority related to the type of crown they

---

[9] Philippians 2:11

are. Therefore, if someone has received a Crown of Sickness, that crown will begin to manifest sickness of some sort in the person's body. As we learn to facilitate the exchange of inferior crowns with Superior Crowns, healing will manifest because a Crown of Wholeness carries with it the authority to release wholeness into a person, thereby defeating the operation of the Crown of Sickness.

> *Crowns are representative of the authority we carry in a particular arena.*

When you read authority-related verses, understand that the inferior is bowing to the superior. As the sons exercise the authority in the various crowns they carry, many who have been weighed down under the weight of inferior crowns will find those crowns coming off their heads and being replaced by a Superior Crown.

Every capability of the Father can be released and made resident in a crown. For healing, we have the expression of Jehovah Raphe (The Lord our Healer), for provision (Jehovah Jireh), for victory in battle, Jehovah Sabaoth (the Lord of Hosts), and more. His touch is in everything He has created. The crowns lack nothing.

> *You are responsible for the stewardship of the blessing contained in a particular crown.*

As you learn to walk and work *from the authority of a Superior Crown,* much will change. When you look in a mirror, see yourself carrying Superior Crowns.

In Luke 10:19, Jesus is speaking and says:

> *Look, I have given you authority (of a Superior Crown) over **all** the power (inferior crowns) of the enemy, and you can walk among snakes and scorpions (operations of inferior crowns) and crush them. Nothing will injure you. (NLT) (Emphasis and additions mine)*

Have you noticed that when we lay hands on someone to pray for them, we generally lay hands upon their head? We are essentially crowning them with whatever it is you are praying for them about or imparting to them. Parents, I suggest you draw your children close and begin to remove any inferior or false crowns you detect, replacing them with the Superior Crowns of Heaven. Teach your children to maintain their crowns by being aware of when the enemy tries to steal them. Also, teach them to access the Court of Crowns for themselves and gain the crowns Heaven wants for them.

These changes can apply to every area of your life. Parents, step into the Court of Crowns and receive what Heaven has for you, and receive the authority of the Superior Crowns. As sons, demonstrate a superior Kingdom. The time is now!

———— ∞ ————

Chapter 15
Strategies of Hell Against Crowns

It should not be a surprise to anyone that, with the release of new revelations on crowns, Hell has been trying to strategically work against this revelation. But first, Heaven wanted us to know that we can step into the Court of Crowns and receive *all* of the Godly crowns that Heaven has designed for us.

We need to repent for *not* picking up the crowns that we were due to have up to this point in our lives. Additionally, we need to repent for placing a false label on a crown. What do I mean by that?

Satan sometimes places false labels on crowns so that the crown is no longer desirable to us. He may imply that, "You don't want that crown, it's too hard," or "it will cost too much," or "It doesn't do what you think." He is simply nefarious like that. With the Crown of Knowledge, he was placing a false label on it (such as "heretic") so that we would not pick up that crown.

Instead, we need the angels of Heaven to remove every false label that has ever been placed on any of our crowns and request the strength of that crown to be restored in full.

The reason someone cannot detect the false label is that the veil over their spiritual eyes clouds their vision, and they cannot determine whether it is the crown's title or a false label on the crown. The image was of someone picking up a crown, trying it on, and then putting it down. They would keep only the ones they wanted, whereas we should want all the Kingdom of Heaven has for us.

Heaven wanted to unveil some of that to us, and in the engagement with Heaven, three books were presented before us. The first book was "Strategies of Hell: How the Enemy Uses Strategies Against Each Crown."

The second book was "Removing the False Labels on Our Crowns". We need to repent for the generations that picked up a crown from heaven, only to see the false label placed upon it by the veil of the spirit of religion, which had been placed upon each of these Godly crowns.

Once we have repented, we need to step into the realms of Heaven and see all the Godly crowns available to the sons and recognize any false labels that the enemy has put upon these crowns: the label of heretic on some crowns, even those that were martyred. It was the crown that was labeled heretic, and the person had to endure much suffering. As sons, without the veil of religion hindering our sight, we can detect the false label and take those false labels off the Godly crowns. The cost has been paid. We don't have to consider the cost.

The third book was titled "Receiving Every Crown of Heaven Available to the Sons." This book is about stepping into the Court of Crowns and receiving every crown of Heaven that is available to the sons. Also, to repent for the generations for picking up a crown that was from Heaven and seeing the false label from the veil of the spirit of religion that had been placed upon each of these Godly crowns, and rejecting that crown.

How do we deal with this?

1. Step into the realms of Heaven and into the Court of Crowns.
2. Acknowledge that we viewed the crowns with the label through the veil of the spirit of religion.
3. Repent.
4. Ask that the veil be removed so that we can see clearly.
5. Receive the crowns.

Court Scenario

As a son, I request access to the Court of Crowns.

I repent where I have viewed Heaven's crowns through the veil of religion. I come out of agreement with the spirit of religion and the veil it imposes upon my life. I would like to have all the crowns that you have available for us as your son.

I request that the false labels be removed.

I request that the false labels on every crown I picked up be removed from these crowns. I request reauthorization of the true purpose of this crown to be released, along with all its aspects.

I also repent for our generations that embraced false labels and viewed crowns through the spirit of religion. I ask for Your forgiveness. I ask that the veil be removed from my generations, and every false label removed.

I receive every crown you have intended for me and my generations with joy!

Thank you.

———— ∞ ————

Chapter 16
Retrieving Lost Crowns

To maximize what Heaven provides through a crown, we need to understand those provisions. The typical components of a crown include:

- **The Crown** – The obvious representation of the authority you carry in the particular arena your crown encompasses.
- **The Mantle** – Coupled with the Anointing, this is the empowerment of Heaven for what your Crown represents and provides.
- **The Throne** – The seated place of your dominion.
- **The Anointing** that accompanies the crown. It is proof of the authorization of the Crown by Heaven.
- **The Scepter** – a secondary symbol of your Throne.
- **The Dominion** that the crown represents.

- **The Glory** – the expression of Heaven that you carry as you wear your crown.
- **The Resources** – the natural and supernatural things you will need to accomplish the mantle of a crown.

I'll discuss these in greater depth later.

If Satan gets your crown he gets all the above.

If you drive on the highway and have a flat tire, you don't abandon the vehicle. You change the tire and continue to your destination. It's the same in our Christian walk. If we make a mistake, it's a temporary setback, not a permanent condition. So you messed up. Repent, get up, and go on. The enemy will say that you have disqualified yourself from all the Father has for you, which may be true as long as the setback is not repented. However, once it is repented of, move on. Don't even pause. Move forward without hesitation!

Setbacks that are unrepented of **will** diminish your authority, but once repented of, the authority is restored in full force. Recognize that the enemy uses those occasions to try to steal your crown. If it got knocked askew, repent, and place it firmly back on your head. Then, request the re-authorization of the authority of that crown.

Revelation 1:5:

May this grace and peace of Jesus Christ overwhelm you. He is the first born from the dead and embodies the evidence and testimony of everything that God believes about you. He heads up the authority in which we reign as kings on the earth. **His crown endorses our crown.** *He always loves us and loosed us once and for all from the dominion of sin in the shedding of his blood. (MIRROR) (Emphasis mine)*

Because Jesus wears His crown, you are fully qualified to wear your crown. He paid the price, he paved the way.

He bought your victory IN FULL at the resurrection.

The Mirror Translation says in Revelation 3:11:

Remember that <u>you</u> call the shots; <u>you</u> wear the crown. Don't let anyone steal your crown! (MIRROR) (Emphasis mine)

You choose to deal with the setbacks and move forward. Heaven isn't stopping you, and hell CANNOT stop you! Only *you* can stop you.

WEAR YOUR CROWN!

If you find these things difficult, it may be that Satan has already stolen some crowns from you:

- A Crown of Fortitude
- A Crown of Hope
- A Crown of Strength
- A Crown of Determination
- A Crown of Overcomer

Let's get them back!

Where we contributed to the loss or forfeiture, we must repent and then go to the Court of Crowns to receive renewed authorization for the authority that had been lost. Request that of the court, having repented for losing that crown. Then, commission the angels to begin bringing in what has been lost and fill the capacity. That capacity can also be enlarged.

Stephanie prayed:

I request access to the Court of Crowns.

Your Honor, where I laid down my authority, or my generations did, and stepped out of our authority, I want to acknowledge that and take responsibility for it. I repent of it and ask that the authority and territory taken be re-established in the name of Jesus.

Where others were involved in the loss or theft of our crowns, I forgive them, bless them, and release them. I ask for the restoration of the crowns.

I ask this court for renewed authorization of the authority that was lost due to the forfeiture or loss of our crown(s).

I also thank the court for the establishment and the capacity of the promised land that have not been able to come forth because of us not governing correctly as sons, but I now understand the capacity of what I am and whose I am as I indeed take in the territory, the lands, the inheritances, and all that has been established here in the name of Jesus.

I commission the angels to bring these things from this place into the natural realm on behalf of the sons, so that I might be a good steward of what you give me.

As Stephanie prayed, she gained a bird's-eye view of the Court of Crowns and realized they were inside a crown.

Retrieval of Lost, Forfeited, or Stolen Crowns

You need to determine if Satan has stolen crowns from you and those in your family. How? Simply ask. Has Satan stolen crowns from me/my spouse/my children?

The answer should be simple to determine. "Yes, or no?" If yes, which I'm sure it will be, then begin to specify various crowns that you feel were taken from you. You could also do this from within the Court of Crowns by observing your personal *Book of Crowns*. You may also find that crowns are displayed in the Trophy Room of Hell.

Once you have a sense of what you have lost due to his thievery, here are the steps of retrieval:

1. Access the Court of Crowns.
2. Repent for our part in the loss of the crown(s)
3. Request the restoration of those crowns you lost.
4. Commission angels to retrieve the crowns from the trophy room of hell and bring them to you.
5. Take them from the angels.
6. Put them on your head.
7. Request the re-authorization of those crowns upon your life.
8. Commission angels to retrieve what was lost or stolen from you, from the north, south, east, west, and every age, realm, and dimension.

Finally, we must understand that a continual association with the victory Jesus purchased for us is necessary to maintain your crown(s).

Revelation 3:12:

*It is in your individual, **continual association with your**[10] **victory in me** that I will make you to be like a strong pillar in the inner shrine of God's sanctuary, supporting the entire structure of my God-habitation within you. A place to be your permanent abode from whence you will never have to depart. And I will engrave upon you the name of my God, also the name of the city [the bride] of my God, the new Jerusalem that descends from heaven; as well as my own new Name. (MIRROR) (Emphasis mine)*

∞
---

[10] A continual, habitual victory

Chapter 17
Crown of Communion

Our engagement on this day was shortly before Passover, and Heaven was preparing to celebrate. As Passover and Resurrection Day approach, the celebrations intensify. As we sat down at the table before us in the Library of Revelation, crowns were at each seat. Stephanie began to see a series of images flashing rapidly before her eyes.

The scene kept changing from her family to her friends and others she would want to invite to sit at the table with us. She understood that the crowns in front of us were the Crowns of Communion for each of us.

She began to realize that this communion is broader than what we take as literal communion with bread and wine, but it is a picture of communion with one another. The Father's plan all along was communion with Him and with one another. Unity of family, not just blood relatives, but family, friends, and community. This was the original design.

As she observed, Stephanie saw different people sitting at the same table. The people would shift from one group to another in an instant. This was the Father's original design.' Communion is an imperative part of *our* design as individuals. John the Revelator had joined us, and he picked up the Crown of Communion on the table in front of him and placed it on his head. He explained that Communion with family and close friends had become a disaster, and the Father seeks to restore communion within the Body of Christ. He sets a time to recognize and honor the body and blood of Jesus, as it is imperative. This communion is with and for each other within the Body. The Body has been deeply divided and broken, beginning with and through the spirit of religion, bringing division, offense, carelessness, accusations, sin, and iniquity. Father's desire is for the sons to walk in communion with one another.

John explained that receiving and wearing the Crown of Communion would help heal the divides because the community of the Body of Christ is broken, and the Father is beginning *to make reparations for community, communion, faith, hope, and love within and between families*. He encouraged us to take our crown. Understand that the Lord has already been preparing your family, and because He loves, it will abound.

Take time this Passover season to reflect on His death, burial, and resurrection, and be mindful of the Crown of Communion. Remember the price that He paid once and for all, as His heart's desire is community and family, *and* He's longing for the original design to be brought into the hearts of men. Seek the Kingdom of God and His righteousness first, and all of these things shall be added unto you. This body of believers (Sandhills Ecclesia, LifeSpring) has sought the Kingdom of God and His righteousness. Boldly take the Crown of Communion and remember.

John exited, and someone else came and sat at the table that Stephanie did not immediately recognize. They reached over and took her by the arm. It was a young man. Still not realizing who it was, she looked deeper and discovered it was her son, the one she had aborted many years prior. She had seen him in Heaven on previous occasions, but never at the age she perceived him that day. She was joyfully taken aback.

He said, "I am being restored to you through Communion." She began to realize she could have communion with those in Heaven when she stepped into Heaven, she could call their spirits forth, just as we sometimes do when conducting court cases. We can have them sit down with us and share communion.

I suggested, "He may have a strategy for your daughters and your new son-in-law." A friend engaged with Heaven, and her father met with her, giving her prayer strategies for her sons.

As she sat with her son, she realized that she had taken away from him the relationships he would have had with his sisters and with his mother, grandmother, and father. All these relationships had been torn from him due to the abortion.

Her son said, "You can bring their spirits here. Those who have lost loved ones can find communion here at the table. It's a table prepared in the presence of your enemies. Restoration and communion do make the enemy angry."

As he said the last phrase, Stephanie noticed, through what seemed to be a window from another dimension, that the enemy was watching her conversation with her son. He was fuming with anger. As it says in Psalm 23:5:

> *You prepare a table before me in the presence of my enemies; You anoint my head with oil; my cup runs over.*

Her son added, "Mom, it wasn't until you took the Crown of Communion that you could see this. Help others to know. Help others to see that, Mom."

He continued, "To be able to walk into the realms of Heaven, to have communion and community here, in Heaven, is the real deal. It's greater than anything you could think or imagine, the way and manner that you can come here and experience it."

Stephanie remarked, "I want that. I know that when I call the spirits of my children and my mother into Heaven, I will bless them and put the armor of God on them. I know that my son is going to have communion with them and that all of us who have loved ones in Heaven can come to the table. I can't wait to tell them this. Thank you, son."

Now, pause, request access to the Court of Crowns, and receive your Crown of Communion. You may want to call someone you love to sit with you in Heaven at the table and share communion. It is life-changing!

Those you call the spirits of into Heaven don't have to be told what you are doing. Their spirit will know, even though their soul may be puzzled. Wait for the testimonies that will eventually come forth from this "dream (or daydream) I had" or something similar. Enjoy the communion.

———— ∞ ————

Chapter 18
Helpful Assistance

No doubt you could read through the lists of questions under the category of Identifying the False Crowns and identify crowns on those in your family, but we don't just need to look at the family. Some prayers and court work will also be required for other influencers in your family's lives.

For example, you want your spouse and children surrounded by Godly friends and confidants. We want those advisors to provide wise, Godly counsel. We want our family shielded from those who would give wicked or worldly counsel.

Prophetic Intercessors

We need prophets who can advise our families on strategies against us, such as what happened in 2 Kings 6:8-12:

> *⁸ Once when the king of Syria was warring against Israel, he took counsel with his servants, saying, 'At such and such a place shall be my camp.'*
>
> *⁹ But the man of God sent word to the king of Israel, 'Beware that you do not pass this place, for the Syrians are going down there.' ¹⁰ And the king of Israel sent to the place about which the man of God told him. Thus he used to warn him, so that he saved himself there more than once or twice. ¹¹ And the mind of the king of Syria was greatly troubled because of this thing, and he called his servants and said to them, 'Will you not show me who of us is for the king of Israel?'*
>
> *¹² And one of his servants said, 'None, my lord, O king; but* **Elisha, the prophet who is in Israel, tells the king of Israel the words that you speak in your bedroom.'** ***(Emphasis mine)***

May these men and women with no agenda other than serving the Father faithfully arise and assist your family.

Angelic Forces

As we pray for our family members, we want the angels of Heaven involved. We want their personal angels on duty, and our family angel alert and on duty.

We want them patrolling their bridges and gates and helping them fulfill their scroll.

Hopefully, your family is surrounded by a Godly support system of Godly men and women, boys and girls.

As we perform this intercession, we will need to activate the angels of our co-workers, bosses, teachers, and others, and commission these angels to accomplish the will of the Father.

You may need to activate them for the person you are praying for, who may have no concept of angels or of co-laboring with their angels. You can help their angels get activated and duly commissioned. Those who have experienced divorce also need the angels of their exes activated so they can help the former spouse cooperate with what Heaven is doing.

For those who are widowed, particularly women, you need Heaven to provide a male support system to assist you with household things as well as to help in the raising of your children. This does not need to be a romantic association, which sometimes merely muddies the water. Children need Godly role models in their lives.

Realize that some of those in your family and support system may have angels who need respite. Request backup angels to be assigned until the primary angels are recovered enough to return to duty.

Occasionally, you may need to request replacements for their angels from the Court of Angels, as some may not be able to fulfill their duties sufficiently. If you notice, in your intercessions, someone who has constant assaults, and their angels always seem to be bested by the attacks, they either need additional help or replacement, or both. Utilizing their angels to assist in the work is invaluable. This is a rare occurrence, but it is essential to be aware of the possibility.

In addition, you want your angels co-laboring with the angels assigned to your children's school, including their teachers, administrators, and their classroom. One of the best ways to co-labor with these angels is to pray in the spirit for them. That will help them by providing the direction of Heaven for them.

You may want to find out the name of some of these angels so you can co-labor with them in a more targeted fashion.

These angels are ready to fulfill the Word of the Lord. Many times, they are simply awaiting instructions from the saints. Not every instruction for angels comes directly from Heaven. Some instructions come through the sons who know how to cooperate with Heaven and with the Angels.

Patrollers

Patrollers are men and women in white who roam geographical areas like scouts, observing the activities in those areas to deliver information to the saints. You can read about some in Zechariah 1. You can engage the patrollers over specific areas to gather intelligence on events that require the angels to be released or intercession in a particular area. I have more information in my book *Engaging the Courts for Your City*.[11] Some of these patrollers can also help you be aware of traps set for your family members, so you can take care of those traps and tricks of the enemy.

Watchers

Additionally, Heaven has watchers (angels who oversee a region's landscape) assigned to aid in the work. Most teaching about watchers is focused on evil watchers. They both perform similar functions, one for the Kingdom of God and the other for Satan.

These Godly watchers can also be consulted for intelligence about the enemy's plans in a particular area or against your family. Don't overlook them. Co-labor with them.

---

[11] *Engaging the Courts for Your City* by Dr. Ron M. Horner. LifeSpring Publishing (2019).

Role Models

Having Godly role models for families is quite beneficial. You and your spouse need them, as do your children or grandchildren. Ask Heaven to provide some Godly role models for your family members.

Some readers of this book have been able to effectively help their family with their crowns and with angelic commissioning. You may consider assisting other families in your community with these concepts by serving as a role model for them and their family members.

———— ∞ ————

Chapter 19
Fruit Inspectors

As you look at the societal landscape, it is clear that some families have given themselves wholly over to many of the false crowns we discussed earlier. It is not our aim to judge them, but it is apparent what crowns some are wearing, and it is imperative that we, as sons, know how to intercede for them effectively.

Matthew 12:33:

Either make the tree good and its fruit good, or else make the tree bad and its fruit bad; for a tree is known by its fruit.

The question to ask is, "Whom do we start with?" Ask for the strategy of Heaven. Once you know who your intercession's focus should be, begin identifying what false crowns they are wearing that need to be replaced with Superior Crowns. Part of this process will be calling them back to where they should be as sons.

Their sin has caused them to miss the mark and forfeit the prize.

They have received a Crown of Authority, as have we all, but what is that crown filled with? Does it have an overflow of the Glory of God, or is it filled with the vileness of hell? Some have made ungodly trades or other factors to get where they are. We must separate the man or woman from their deeds. We need to see who they really are before the family. If you don't love them, however, stop praying for them. You will pray incorrectly for them. Ask the Father for love for them. Ask Him to help you see them as He sees them. You may perform some acts of kindness on their behalf.

Jude had this counsel for us to consider in Jude 1:17-23:

> *[17] But you, beloved, remember the words which were spoken before by the apostles of our Lord Jesus Christ: [18] how they told you that there would be mockers in the last time who would walk according to their own ungodly lusts.*
>
> *[19] These are sensual persons, who cause divisions, not having the Spirit.*
>
> *[20] But you, beloved, building yourselves up on your most holy faith, praying in the Holy Spirit, [21]* **keep yourselves in the love of God,** *looking for the mercy of our Lord Jesus Christ unto eternal life. [22] And* **on some have compassion,**

> *making a distinction; ²³ but others save with fear, pulling them out of the fire, hating even the garment defiled by the flesh.* (Emphasis mine)

Those opting for false and inferior crowns haven't been introduced to the goodness of the Father. They don't know Him like you do...yet.

Understanding the significant influences our family members face by recognizing the false crowns will help us in removing those false influences. We want them replaced with Godly crowns. We also want to see their Crown of Authority filled with the Glory of Heaven rather than the vileness that some are filled with now. Don't forget to place the Crown of Everlasting upon their heads to help awaken them to the goodness of the Father.

We want to see the change mentioned in Malachi 4:6 modeled in our families:

> *And he will turn the hearts of the fathers to the children, and the hearts of the children to their fathers.*

Although everyone has a Crown of Authority, many have their crown filled with the wrong substance. We want our crowns to be filled with the Glory and substance of the Father. When we see someone, whose crown is contaminated by darkness, we can repent on their behalf, forgive their sins, and request their crown be cleansed and filled with the Glory of Heaven.

When we see someone wearing a Crown of Loathing, we can repent on their behalf, forgive them their sins, and request that the wrap-around love of God be poured into their lives, replacing the Crown of Loathing with a Crown of Grace and a Crown of the Love of the Father.

Those wearing a Crown of Fear, like those with a Crown of Loathing, need it replaced with a Crown of the Wrap-around Love of the Father. Apply these patterns to those wearing the false crowns of the seven-headed dragon, so that they may experience the love and might of God in their lives.

People don't serve God because they don't know God. To know Him is to love Him.

The work of familial intercession is to align the members of a family with the purposes of Heaven. Over the last several years, forces have been at work to destroy family units. It's time for the sons to arise, step into their governing role, and legislate from the Courts of Heaven the purposes of God for our country and the families within our country.

When we, through the perception of our spirit, look at a father, mother (or other caregiver), or child, ask what the Father has for them. Regardless of what their crowns are filled with, the Father has a plan for them. Some are precisely where they are supposed to be. Others have been taken off course. May our intercession lead to a course correction in their life, enabling them to fulfill God's purposes.

———— ∞ ————

Chapter 20
Maintaining Your Crown

John, the revelator gave us some great insights in how to maintain our crown in Revelation 3:11-12:

¹¹ Do not let tough times make me seem distant from you. I am at hand—see my nearness, not my absence. And don't let temporal setbacks diminish your own authority either. Remember that <u>you call the shots; you wear the crown</u>. My crown endorses your crown. (Lit. Let nothing take your crown.

¹² It is in your individual, continual association with your victory in me that I will make you to be like a strong pillar in the inner shrine of God's sanctuary, supporting the entire structure of my God-habitation within you. A place to be your permanent abode 'from whence you will never have to depart. And I will engrave upon you the name of my God, also the name of the city [the bride.] of my God, the new Jerusalem that descends from heaven; as well as my own new Name. (MIRROR)

Here are some points to consider:

1. Stay Present to His Nearness

[11] Do not let tough times make Me seem distant from you. I am at hand—see My nearness, not My absence.

Insight

- Hard seasons can **cloud your awareness** of God's presence.
- But Jesus reminds us: **He is close**, especially in the struggle.
- Maintaining your crown begins with **maintaining your connection**—staying anchored in intimacy, not circumstances.

How to Apply

- Refuse to interpret delay or pain as abandonment.
- Practice awareness of His nearness in daily life.
- Speak to your soul: *"He is not far. He is here. He is faithful."*

2. Guard Your Authority

¹¹ Don't let temporal setbacks diminish your own authority either. Remember that you call the shots; you wear the crown. (Lit. "Let no one take your crown.")

Insight

- Crowns represent spiritual authority, identity, and reward.
- Setbacks, criticism, or self-doubt can erode our sense of God-given rule. They are designed to chip away at your assuredness of your authority. Delay is not denial.
- Jesus reminds us that your crown is active <u>now</u>, not just in the age to come.

How to Apply

- Don't hand over your crown through **passivity, fear, or compromise**.
- When attacked, remind yourself: *"I wear a crown. I carry Heaven's backing."*
- **Speak** with authority. **Pray** with confidence. **Walk** like royalty.

---

3. Stand Secure in Union with Christ

¹² It is in your individual, <u>continual association</u> with your victory in Me...

Insight

- Union with Christ is not a one-time moment—it is a **continual, living connection**.
- Victory flows **from Him to you**, not from your effort alone.

How to Apply

- Rehearse your identity daily: "As He is, so am I in this world."[12]
- Refuse **shame, fear,** or **separation-based thinking**.
- **Celebrate your shared victory** with Christ every day. You are co-raised and co-seated.

---

4. Become a Pillar in His Sanctuary

[12] I will make you to be like a strong pillar in the inner shrine...

Insight

- Become unmovable
- You're not just visiting God's presence—you're becoming part of His dwelling. *In you He lives and moves and has His being. (Acts 17:28)*

---

[12] 1 John 4:17

- A pillar supports weight and brings stability—this is a reward of endurance.

How to Apply

- See yourself as a **fixed part of God's house**, not a guest or outsider.
- Endurance today **builds spiritual stature** tomorrow.
- You are **a supporting structure** in the Father's Kingdom on Earth.

---

5. Receive His Names Written on You (Stay firm in your identity, which is found in Him.

[12] I will engrave upon you the name of My God... the city of My God... and My own new Name.

Insight

- These engravings speak of **ownership**, **belonging**, and **intimacy**.
- To maintain your crown is to walk **branded by Heaven**, carrying its identity and authority.

How to Apply

- Declare, "I am marked by God. I belong to Heaven. His Name is on me."
- Let your life reveal His nature—His character etched in your actions.

- You are not nameless—you are named **by the King.**

Summary: How to Maintain Your Crown

Principle	**Action**
Stay near	Don't let trials blind you to His presence
Guard your crown	Walk in your God-given authority, don't forfeit it
Abide in victory daily	Stay joined to Christ's triumph
Be unshakable	Let endurance make you a pillar in God's house
Live marked	Carry His Name, His city, and His Glory on your life

Activation Prayer

Father, thank You for placing a crown upon my head—a crown of righteousness, life, and glory.

Teach me to walk worthy of it.

I repent for any time I have dishonored or neglected what You entrusted to me.

By Your grace, I choose to hold fast, walk in humility, and live faithfully before You.

Help me to endure, to resist temptation, and to honor You in everything.

May no one take my crown, in Jesus' name, Amen.

――――― ∞ ―――――

Chapter 21
Epilogue

Many believers have lost the strength that comes with the crowns they once possessed. I discussed how to regain lost, forfeited, or stolen crowns. This book was about embracing the crown's understanding on behalf of your family and maximizing these crowns. Since the focus of this book has been familial intercession, we must know the answer to the following question:

How do we apply the understanding of crowns and familial intercession?

As we have received the full activation of our Crown of Authority and our Crown of Family Intercession, these will provide the resources to begin the work:

1. Ask Heaven for greater love for those you are praying for.
2. Gain access to the Court of Crowns.
3. Ask for the strategy of Heaven.

4. Identify the false crowns at work in the lives of those in your family.
5. Begin the repentance work (use the various Court Scenarios provided in this book).
6. Get the false and ungodly crowns removed from them.
7. Petition Heaven on their behalf for the Superior Crowns of Heaven for them.
8. Get them placed upon their heads.
9. Go to the next person and continue the process.

Once you have completed this for your immediate family, begin this work on behalf of the influencers in your extended family, coworkers, students, or others. Keep tabs on the progress made within your family so they can all maximize what Heaven has in store.

May your spouse, children, grandchildren, and others you love experience the riches of Heaven provided through the crowns.

———— ∞ ————

Appendix

Learning to Live Spirit First

A challenge with how we were taught about the Christian life is that everything was put off until sometime in the future. Then, we read Paul's letters and experienced a disconnect. Heaven, to us, was a destination, not a resource. We knew nothing about learning to live from our spirits. We only knew what we had been doing since birth, and that was to live to satisfy our soul or flesh. We sorely need to learn an alternative way of living.

Exchanging Our Way of Living

Paul recorded these words in his letter to the Romans:

Romans 8:5:

> *Those who are motivated by the flesh only pursue what benefits themselves. But those who live by the impulses of the Holy Spirit are motivated to pursue spiritual realities.*

We must learn to live spirit first! We must exchange our way of living. We must learn to live from our spirit. We need to understand the hierarchy within us:

    a. We are a spirit.
    b. We possess a soul.
    c. We live in a body.

Each component has a specific purpose in our lives. Our spirit is the interface with the supernatural realm. It is designed for interfacing with Heaven and the Kingdom realm. Our spirit has been in existence in our body since conception. Our soul has a different purpose. It communicates to our intellect and our physical body what our spirit has obtained from Heaven. It is the interface with our body. Our body houses the two components and follows the dictates of whichever component is dominating,

Most of us have never been taught about having our spirit dominate. Rather, we have merely assumed that our soul being dominant was the required mode of operation.

Our soul always wants to be in charge. Our soul is susceptible to carnal or fleshly desires, lusts, and behaviors. It will, at times, resist our spirit and body. It must be made to submit to our spirit by an act of our will.

Our will is a means of instructing either component (spirit, soul, or body) in what to do. Our soul has a will, and so does our spirit. We choose who dominates!

Our body, on the other hand, has appetites that will control us in subjection to our soul. They become partners in crime—remember that second piece of chocolate cake it wanted? Our body will try, along with our soul, to dictate our behavior. It will likely resist the spirit's domination of our lives. However, it will obey our spirit's domination if instructed, and our body can aid our spirit if trained to do so.

The typical expression that operates in most people's lives is that their soul is first, body second, and their spirit is somewhere in the distance in last place.

In some people, especially those very conscious of their physical fitness or physical appearance, there is a different lineup. Their body is their priority, the soul second, and again, their spirit is the lowest priority.

Heaven's desire for us is vastly different. Heaven desires that we live spirit first, soul second, and body third. Since we are spiritual beings, this is the optimal arrangement. For most of us, our spirit was not activated in our lives in any measure until we became born again.

If, after our salvation experience, we began to pursue our relationship with the Father, then we became much more aware of our spirit and learned to live more spirit-conscious. The apostle Paul wrote in his various epistles about living in the spirit or walking in the spirit.

> *Because we are spiritual beings, our spirits cry out for a deepening of relationship with the Father.*

Our spirit longs for it and will try to steer us in that direction. Many of us had a hunger for God from early in our lives.

Our soul has certain characteristics that explain its behavior in our life. This is the briefest of lists, but I think we will get the idea. Our soul is selfish. It wants what it wants when it wants it. It can be very pouty. It can act like a small child. It is offendable and often even looks for opportunities to be offended. Our soul is also rude.

Our body has a different set of characteristics. It is inconsiderate, demanding, lazy, and self-serving. It does not want to get out of bed in the morning, for many people. In others, it wants to be fed things that are not beneficial.

However, the characteristics of our spirit are hugely different. If we live out of our spirit, we will find that we are loving and prone to be gentle. We desire peace. We are considerate. We are far more contented when living out of our spirit. Also, joy will often have a great expression in our lives.

Sometimes, we have experienced traumas that create a situation of our soul not trusting our spirit. The soul blames the spirit for not protecting it. The irony is that, typically, our soul never gave place to the spirit so that it could protect us. The soul places false blame on the spirit, and it must be coerced to forgive the spirit. Then, the soul must relinquish control to the spirit. Once the soul forgives the spirit, the two components can begin to work in harmony.

If I were to flash an image of some delicious, freshly cooked donuts in front of us, what would happen? For many, their body would announce a craving for one. What if, instead, I showed an image of a bowl of broccoli? How many people would get excited about that? Probably not as much excitement over a bowl of broccoli would be exhibited. Which does our body prefer—the donuts or broccoli? For the untamed soul, the donuts are likely to win out every time. Which do most kids prefer?

In any case, we can train ourselves to go for the healthier option. A principle regarding this that I heard years ago is summed up like this:

> *What we feed will live—*
> *what we starve will die*

What do we want to be dominant—our spirit, our soul, or our body? The part we feed is the part that will dominate.

For some, they feed their soul and live by the logic of their mind. Everything must be reasoned out in their mind before they will accept it. However, because our soul gains its insight from the Tree of the Knowledge of Good and Evil, it will always have faulty and limited understandings.

How do we change this soul-dominant or body-dominant pattern? We instruct our soul to back up, and we call our spirit to come forward. Some people may need to physically stand up and speak to our soul and say, "Soul, back up," and as they say those words, take a physical step backward. Then, speak to their spirit out loud and say, "Spirit, come forward." As we speak those words, take a physical step forward. This prophetic act helps trigger a shift within them.

Live spirit first!

Benefits of Living Spirit First

Why would we want to live spirit first? Let me present several reasons. Living spirit first will create in us an increased awareness of Heaven and the realms of Heaven. It will create a deeper comprehension of the presence of Holy Spirit, of angels, and men and women in white linen. We will be able to better hear the voice of Heaven. We will experience greater creativity, productivity, hope, and peace. We will become more aware of the needs of people that we meet.

> *As we live spirit first,*
> *we will be able to access*
> *the riches of Heaven in our life.*

Petty things that formerly bothered us will dissipate in importance or impact in our lives. We will be able to move ahead, not concerned with the petty, mundane, or unproductive things that have affected our lives before we begin to live spirit first.

This way of life is more than a game changer—for the believer, it is the only way to live. We will face challenges as we build our business or live our lives from Heaven down, but we will more readily be able to access the solutions of Heaven as we live with an awareness of the richness of Heaven and all that is available to us as sons or daughters of the Lord Most High. Do not live dominated by the soul.

> *Live **spirit** first!*

———— ∞ ————

Resources from LifeSpring International Ministries

A visit to the **RonHorner.com** website will give a glimpse of the various branches of ministry we are involved in. We started by providing coaching to people within the Courts of Heaven, advocating for them and their situations. Our corporate name is LifeSpring International Ministries, Inc., a North Carolina registered nonprofit.

Personal Advocacy Sessions

Known as Personal Advocacy Sessions, these 90-minute sessions with our trained team of advocates have successfully worked with a myriad of situations. If you have an issue that you can't seem to get breakthrough about, schedule a session with our advocates.

LifeSpring Mentoring Group

Since starting this weekly class on Zoom in 2019, we have taught on the Courts of Heaven, protocols, engaging Heaven for revelation, working with angels and men and women in white linen, lingering human spirits, and more. It is a free class. Simply visit **ronhorner.com** to register for the link for the class.

Membership Program

We have several tiers of membership for those tracking with us. The Platinum level gains you access to our library of videos, blogs, and more. Again, visit the website.

LifeSpring School of Ministry

A trimester-based school to help you grow in your walk. Trimester 1 focuses on cleansing your generations. Trimester 2 focuses on Protocols of the Courts of Heaven, and Trimester 3 focuses on Advanced Protocols of the Courts of Heaven. Completion of Trimesters 1, 2, and 3 will qualify the student for consideration as a Junior or Senior Advocate able to conduct Personal Advocacy Sessions with our clients.

CourtsNet

CourtsNet is our video-based training program offering a wide variety of classes and courses. We have free courses as well as paid courses.

AfterCare

Not every situation is solved by the Courts of Heaven. Sometimes people need to learn simple things to navigate life. Our AfterCare program provides Biblical counseling, classes, and groups regularly.

Sandhills Ecclesia

In 2022, we began a Sunday Gathering known as Sandhills Ecclesia, which is the name we saw on the book in Heaven when we went to inquire. My wife, Adina, and I live in the North Carolina area known as the Sandhills region, hence the name. We meet weekly at 11:00 AM Eastern Time, and on the first Sunday of each month, we have an afternoon gathering to conduct legislative work in the Courts of Heaven as a group. All are welcome. Simply visit **sandhillsecclesia.com** and register for the link.

Heaven Down Business

Heaven Down Business is a worldwide coaching and consultancy business designed to assist entrepreneurs and business owners in implementing the Heaven Down™ Business Building paradigm into their business. For more information, visit **heavendownbusiness.com**.

Adina's Melodies/Heaven Down Music

Adina Horner, co-founder, is a gifted minstrel and has several albums of prophetic worship music available on several of the most popular music platforms. Visit **adinasmelodies.com**.

LifeSpring Publishing/Scroll Publishers

LifeSpring Publishing primarily publishes Dr. Ron's books, and Scroll Publishers is our imprint where we publish the books of others relating to engaging Heaven, living spirit forward, and the Heaven Down™ lifestyle.

YouTube Channel

Our most recent videos from the Mentoring Group are posted on YouTube®. Visit our YouTube® channel,

courtsofheavenwebinar on YouTube® for the latest videos.

RonHorner.com

Our website, **RonHorner.com,** has a myriad of resources, many of which are free, as well as numerous videos.

―――― ∞ ――――

Description

Embracing Crowns for Your Family is a heartfelt invitation to step into your divine role as a royal intercessor for your family. This book unveils the truth that your prayers carry weight—not just as hopeful petitions, but as Heaven-backed decrees shaped by the authority of the crown you've been given.

Whether you're contending for a prodigal, standing for generational healing, or simply longing to see your household walk in divine alignment, this guide will equip you with spiritual strategies, biblical insights, and heaven-born confidence.

You were never meant to fight for your family alone. You were designed to govern from a place of love, peace, and power—seated with Christ, crowned with purpose.

Discover how to:

- Break generational cycles and establish blessings

- Intercede from a place of authority, not anxiety
- Partner with Heaven to restore God's design for your family

It's time to take your place, wear your crown, and see your family through Heaven's eyes. The legacy begins with you.

———— ∞ ————

About the Author

Dr. Ron Horner is an apostolic teacher specializing in the Courts of Heaven. He has written nearly forty books on the Courts of Heaven, engaging Heaven, working with angels, living from revelation, and most recently on Crowns of Authority.

He currently trains people in engaging the Courts of Heaven in a weekly online teaching session. You can register to participate and discover more about the Courts of Heaven prayer paradigm on his various websites, classes, products, and services found here:

www.ronhorner.com

Other Books by Dr. Ron M. Horner

Building Your Business from Heaven Down

Building Your Business from Heaven Down 2.0

Building Your Business with the Blueprint of Heaven

Commissioning Angels – Volume 1

Cooperating with The Glory

Courts of Heaven Process Charts

Dealing with Trusts & Consequential Liens

Embracing Crowns for Governmental Intercession

Embracing Crowns for Your Business

Embracing Crowns for Your Family

Embracing Your Crown of Authority

Engaging Angels in the Realms of Heaven

Engaging Heaven for Revelation – Volume 1

Engaging Heaven for Revelation – Volume 2

Engaging Heaven for Trade

Engaging the Courts for Ownership & Order

Engaging the Courts for Your City (*Paperback, Leader's Guide & Workbook*)

Engaging the Courts of Healing & the Healing Garden

Engaging the Courts of Heaven

Engaging the Help Desk of the Courts of Heaven

Four Keys to Dismantling Accusations

Freedom from Mithraism

Kingdom Dynamics – Volume 1

Kingdom Dynamics – Volume 2

Let's Get it Right!

Lingering Human Spirits

Lingering Human Spirits – Volume 2

Living Spirit Forward

Maximizing Your Crown of Authority

Next Dimension Access to the Court of Supplications

Overcoming the False Verdicts of Freemasonry

Overcoming Verdicts from the Courts of Hell

Releasing Bonds from the Courts of Heaven

The Courts of Heaven: An Introduction (formerly *Engaging the Mercy Court of Heaven*)

Unlocking Spiritual Seeing

Working with Your Realms and Your Realm Angels

SPANISH

Cómo Anular los Falsos Veredictos de la Masonería

Cómo Proceder en la Corte Celestial de Misericordia

Cómo Proceder en las Cortes para su Ciudad

Cómo Trabajar con Angeles en los Ambitos del Cielo

Cooperando con La Gloria de Dios

Las Cuatro Llaves para Anular las Acusaciones

Liberando Bonos en las Cortes Celestiales

Liberando Su Visión Espiritual

Sea Libre del Mitraísmo

Tablas de Proceso de la Cortes del Cielo

———— ∞ ————

www.ingramcontent.com/pod-product-compliance
Lightning Source LLC
Chambersburg PA
CBHW021834220426
43663CB00005B/246